Jane Miller first worked in publishing, then as an English teacher in a London comprehensive and finally as a Professor at the London University Institute ~f ~~~~~~~~. Her publications include *Mar~ ~~~~~~~~~~~~~~~~~~~~~~e and Education*; *Women Wri~~~~~~~~~~~~~~~~~~~~~~'es in Reading and Culture*; *S~~~~~~~~~~~~~~~~~~~~~~~Age* and *In My Own Time: T~~~~~~~~~~~~~~~~~~~~~s* in London.

'This is a remarkable collection, a reflection not just of a later life well lived, but a distinct political and personal sensibility. Far from being "over the hill", Miller is one of a growing tribe of female elders who stand right on the peak, taking a wry, wise and witty view of all they survey' *Guardian*

'Jane Miller's collected journalism is a treasure trove of literary, personal and political marvels. The writing is a joy, as is the observation, wit and humanity that underpin it: like Montaigne, only funnier' Matthew d'Ancona, *Guardian* and *Evening Standard* columnist

'Her erudition is both dazzling and lightly borne, the personal often illuminating the political ... Miller's is a welcome, necessary voice – readable, informative and entertaining' *Times Literary Supplement*

'[An] entertaining and insightful collection ... her writing has a fascinating effect: she is forced to look in on herself from the outside. She isn't confined to age, menopause or retirement as themes ... Miller's writing is filled with a wisdom, cheery world-weariness and kindness ... She is wonderful on age and authority ... Miller is a fantastic companion' Viv Groskop, *Telegraph*

In My Own Time
Thoughts and Afterthoughts

Jane Miller

virago

VIRAGO

First published in Great Britain in 2016 by Virago Press
This paperback edition published in 2017 by Virago Press

1 3 5 7 9 10 8 6 4 2

Copyright © Jane Miller 2016

The moral right of the author has been asserted.

A CIP catalogue record for this book
is available from the British Library.

ISBN 978-0-349-00757-1

Typeset in Perpetua by M Rules
Printed and bound in Great Britain by
Clays Ltd, St Ives plc

Papers used by Virago are from well-managed forests
and other responsible sources.

Virago Press
An imprint of
Little, Brown Book Group
Carmelite House
50 Victoria Embankment
London EC4Y 0DZ

An Hachette UK Company
www.hachette.co.uk

www.virago.co.uk

To Karl

Contents

Preface

I became a journalist at the age of seventy-eight. I'd written books, founded and then edited an academic journal called *Changing English* for twenty years, and written articles and reviews, but I'd never felt like a real journalist. In early 2011, some months after I'd published a book called *Crazy Age: Thoughts on Being Old*, I got a message from my publisher that *In These Times*, an American monthly, wanted to use an excerpt from the book. Quite a lot of that book had originally appeared in another American magazine, a quarterly called *Raritan*, but I'd had no offers from an American book publisher, so I was delighted to agree. Not long after that, Joel Bleifuss, the editor of *In These Times*, emailed to ask whether I'd like to write a monthly column for his magazine. I googled the magazine, found that it was described on Wikipedia as 'politically progressive/democratic socialist' and accepted instantly. I also discovered that it was founded in 1976, is published out of Chicago by the Institute for Public Affairs, and has an impressive list of past and present contributors, including E. P. Thompson, Noam Chomsky, Herbert Marcuse, Kurt Vonnegut, Barbara Ehrenreich and Slavoj Žižek.

Joel and I have been emailing each other in laconic style ever since. It's been more than four years. We've never met and we've spoken only once on the phone. I know a few things about him now: that he comes from a long line of socialists, has a Spanish wife, who reads my column, and three grown-up sons. One of them was working in Africa when one of mine was too. He, his assistant editors and volunteers, never mind his readers, have been unknown and invisible to me. I've winged a piece off to him once a month, and it's usually been preceded by a week of panic as I try desperately to think what to write about before finally getting down to it. There is often far too much in the news or in my life, not all of it suitable, though on one or two occasions I could think of nothing at all. Joel sometimes suggests a subject, and until Karl, my husband, died in 2014, he used to read my pieces carefully and make suggestions for the next one, as my son Sam does now.

Karl has edited pretty well everything I've ever written, and going over a piece of writing with him was a bit like a tutorial and might take hours. No emails for him. He never sent or received an email in his life, and he expected you to give him something on paper, on whose margins he made the faintest of pencil marks, in the belief that there was no need in the world to make more than one copy of something that was going to be printed, and pencil marks could be rubbed out. He much preferred his ancient Olivetti to the beautiful Apple desktop computer he was persuaded to buy and which he treated with disdain and as no more than a rogue typewriter with unpleasant habits. We'd sit side by side at the kitchen table. He'd tell me not to get cross, and I'd try not to. Then he'd quietly ask me whether I really meant to say what I'd said at some point, and I almost always took his advice, especially when the answer was 'No'. He rarely told me I was wrong. He simply asked me to explain whether or why I thought I was right: a fine teaching strategy.

Sometimes my email to Joel and its attachment are not acknowledged for an uneasy week or so; but eventually there's a message saying 'Got it', and a little later on there's a second one, returning the piece with colourful lines and emendations that make it look something like a map of the London underground. Though this email seems to come from Joel, it's usually the work of a 'young person' who has found my prose and my grasp of facts wanting in a number of ways. I can make neither head nor tail of the 'track changes' and the colourful insertions. So I'm inclined to give up trying to and beg Joel to tidy it up for me but leave it more or less as it was. Which, astonishingly, he nearly always does. But he gives me good advice, of the 'Journalists tend to write in short paragraphs' kind. There've been times when I felt rather as Helene Hanff must have felt writing to Frank Doel and asking him to send her the books she wanted; letters which were later turned into that wonderful book, *84 Charing Cross Road*. She was asking for books and also for someone who'd make it possible for her to get to London, whether through her reading or in reality. I'm asking Joel for approval and a sense that what I have to say about London and Britain and my own life there might mean something to a reader in America.

Joel gets his young helpers to do a great deal of fact-checking as, I believe, all American magazine editors do. We all fell out on one occasion when I quoted Prince Harry saying what I thought was the most interesting thing I'd ever heard him say: 'Sometimes I'm not sure,' he wondered once in a television programme about him, 'whether I'm a person or a prince'. The remark was cut from my column because it could not be found anywhere on the Internet. Perhaps I did imagine it. But I doubt whether Harry would have taken me to court if I did. He has much more worrying comments to contend with, after all, poor fellow. So I've put it back again here. On another occasion, when I'd written about relations between the old and the young, the fur flew, and I emailed Joel plaintively,

> Joel. I've gone through these comments. Someone thinks I'm a cross old bag who needs editing. I can't deal with it. I wanted to think about the differences. I wasn't trying to suggest that my grandchildren were somehow inferior to me. FAR FROM IT. What do I do?

Joel has a volunteer proof reader of eighty-eight, who has been known to utter 'So what?' after reading one of my pieces, so it isn't only the young who may be sceptical. But I've learned from them all: first, to write something more or less 800 words long, and then on one occasion managing to complete a piece in under two hours, which is a record for me.

Every once in a while Joel compliments me, says a piece is beautiful or funny or interesting, and I'm overjoyed. But when I consider the pieces he likes and the ones he likes quite a lot less I'm at sea. I've tried to work out what he likes. Is it the pieces about books I've been reading or films I've seen or the ones about childhood or youthful memories? Or is it the ones about British politics and scandals? I wrote to him at one point, 'You always like the ones that were hardest to write.' He also likes me to put in the actual names of friends and family, so he must want me to write out of the particular world I inhabit in London in the twenty-first century. I sent him a photograph of Karl reading the paper in our kitchen, and he was particularly interested in the plates and cups on the dresser. He wanted me to write about Karl's illness and then his death and how I was coping with it all. But when I obliged and wrote him a piece and followed it three months later with another, he thought the second one was going too far. I'd felt I had more to say and I said it. So that one is here too. I suppose I'm beginning to understand this journalism business, but it isn't always easy to imagine what Joel's American readers already know about this country or what they'd like to hear about it. I've been told that only 37 per cent of Americans have passports. If that's true there can't be all that many of them who are interested in this country or any other, apart from their own.

I've tried to imagine the office on North Milwaukee

Avenue from which *In These Times* emerges. My last visit to
Chicago was in 1997, when I spoke at a conference there.
The occasion is unpleasantly encapsulated – perhaps I mean
embalmed – for me by the sandwich I bought in the large
international hotel where I was staying, and my horror at
finding a dead fly sitting atop the sandwich, incarcerated
in its death throes within the transparent packet it shared
with what I'd hoped was my lunch. But that's not fair. I
also spent a cool and happy spring morning at Oak Park,
the suburb of Chicago where Frank Lloyd Wright built
houses, including his own, which is now a museum. And I
walked and walked by the lake and elsewhere. My youngest
granddaughter had just been born, and between conference
sessions I wandered up and down Michigan Avenue looking – unsuccessfully – for a shop where I could buy her a
small American garment. I still haven't bought her one and
she is now eighteen and five foot ten.

This may be an appropriate moment to admit that though
I can google and email, just about, I'm not good at these
things, and – ignominiously – I've needed constant help
from the younger generation. One of these indispensables
has now introduced me to something called Google Street
View. So I've finally set eyes on the street and the office of
the magazine and seen the front of the Discount Store next
door, where I could have bought 'clothing for all the family'
for next to nothing all those years ago. I imagine the editor
and his young assistants bicycling efficiently along that wide
road, braced for a day's fact-checking, assembling the magazine and then 'putting it to bed'. Substituting 'sprinkler'

for 'hose pipe' and querying the use of other anglicisms must be the least of their tasks each month.

My son Sam came up with *From the Old Country* as a title for my column. It catches pretty well my life as an old person in London as well as Britain during the last years of coalition government and the first year of the Conservative one after that, with all their scandals and ineptitudes, the austerity, the gigantic bonuses, the galloping inequality and the inexorable destruction of the welfare state: the National Health Service, public education and legal aid. Secretly and immodestly, I thought of my pieces as *Letters to America*, because that's what writing them felt like, an answer of a sort to Alistair Cooke's *Letters from America*. I haven't been to America for a long time, and I can't be sure whether the magazine's readers really want to hear about the particular iniquities and absurdities of the UK, though some of these must be ones they recognise all too well. *In These Times* manages to be optimistic as well as critical in the writing it publishes and in its layout. It contains lots of interesting photographs, and they usually find a good one to put in the middle of my column. So I've included here the pieces I wrote about Occupy and the so-called Arab Spring – though they may seem sadly out of date now – as reminders of that brief moment in 2011 and early 2012, when a youthful politics seemed to be opening like a crocus in February, to be trodden down and forgotten by summertime.

Between October 2011 and September 2012, and in addition to the column, Joel asked me to do some interviews, also something I'd not done before. I've included two of these, with Tony Benn and Eric Hobsbawm, because I was lucky enough to talk to these two distinguished men of the Left not long before they died. These are longer here than they were when Joel published them. It seemed worth including most of what was said for their historical interest. I also interviewed Owen Jones, when he'd just written *Chavs*, and Polly Toynbee of the *Guardian*, an old friend who is also a journalist I hugely admire and wish I could emulate. They are still very much alive, with weekly columns of their own, so I've not included my interviews with them. I am no Polly Toynbee and no Jeremy Paxman, no provocateur or dog with a bone, and I'm probably unduly emollient and fearful of disagreement. Until now I had only interviewed prospective students, and had eventually learned how to wheedle thoughts out of their reticence. Luckily for me, none of my interviewees showed the slightest reticence, and I was impressed by them all and by their determination to work for change in British society and their ability to understand how it might come about. I am, though, quite unable to think of questions, respond to answers *and* manage to record it all. So I took my grandson, Joe, with me to one or two of the interviews and he recorded them in a surprising if symbiotic relation to his own very interesting musical compositions, while offering fierce and anarchic interpellations from time to time. Another grandchild, Roxana, was less inclined to interrupt and if anything even better at the technicalities.

Many years ago I gave my mother the typescript of a book I'd written. She instantly dropped it down by the side

of her bed, and though she retrieved most of it she wondered aloud whether it mattered 'terribly' what order she
read the pages in. 'No,' I replied, 'not terribly, but it might
help.' These pieces may be read in any order, however. I
have arranged them chronologically, as they were written, but they could be read from the back, like a Hebrew
prayer book, or very nearly. I offer these pieces and interviews now as anything but exemplary journalism of the
sort I relish in writers like Joseph Roth, Janet Malcolm or
Andrew O'Hagan, rather as a collection of small windows
on these last four years, which have been turbulent for me
and far more so for most of the rest of the world.

September 2015

Change

This was my first column for Joel, and it seems to me now that I was announcing — perhaps a little apologetically — who I was: confessing that I was middle-class, had attended a school where I didn't learn much, was a bit of a technophobe or technofool, and that I was awash in memories of a sort which might seem dull or incomprehensible to an American readership. Here it is. Joel found this beautiful portrait of Sir George Villiers to go with the piece.

I have a problem with history. Always have had. I went to what was known as a 'progressive' school, on a free place, because my father taught the piano there. In the junior school I learned about the geography and history of Hampshire, the small southern English county we inhabited. I can still draw its outline with my eyes shut. Later on, I learned about Sir George Villiers, father of the first Duke of Buckingham, who lived from 1550 to 1606 and was so dissolute and fathered so many children that it was statistically likely, we were told, that at least one of our class was descended from him.

My history teacher, who later wrote a book called *Uncommon People: A Study of England's Elite*, was contemptuous of convention. He brought his bicycle into the classroom and wore his pyjamas under his coat. He bears at least some responsibility for my difficulty with history

and with change, since he eventually threw me out of his class for behaving, as he put it, like the Queen of Sheba. And that was that. I have had to peg out time with personal dates of my own ever since; 1860, for instance, was the year when my great-aunt Clara was born, and she was fifteen when Karl Marx helped her with her German homework in 1875, and so on.

Yet we old ones ought to be historians of our times, registers of subtle as well as momentous change. My grandchildren, after all, study the Second World War at school, along with the Russian Revolution, and my own children learned of little else during their school and university days but the causes of the First World War, that my father remembered in such detail from his teenage years. We grandparents were there, witnesses to it all; yet I am shaky and uncertain when it comes to change itself and not much good at remembering moments when the world spun on its axis. It's true that I remember dancing to Victor Silvester with my sternly non-dancing father on VE day in May 1945 in the local town hall. But more often time is marked for me by the births of babies, the deaths of my elders or the day in 1985 when I stopped smoking.

My own childhood has acquired the colour-drained, sepia tones of the photographs that document it. Yet what changes there have been! So many wars since the main one, and I do remember my headmistress telling us grimly about the beginning of the Korean War, and of course I remember the Vietnam War and demonstrations against it in Grosvenor Square. But I could not reliably date those

wars, nor the elections and the misjudgements that followed them.

I suppose the most astonishing changes of my lifetime
really are the technological ones. Those young people in
Cairo and in the cities of Libya and Bahrain use the Internet
in ways I don't understand and which surely no one foresaw
even ten years ago. My first 'go' on a computer was in my
university in the late 1980s. I thought of it as a newfangled
typewriter to be shared with my colleagues. Yet, primitive
as it was, and ignorant as I was, the university was well
ahead then of the BBC, where my son worked. I typed out
a chapter of a book I was writing, and was told firmly to
take great care with 'saving' it. I took such care, in fact,
that I saved it many, many times, used up all the computer's
available memory and couldn't, therefore, print a single
copy of it. The chapter, which whirred past me, occasionally punctuated by its title, was called 'An Odd Woman',
as it happens. It took me three or four years to recover my
confidence and buy myself an Amstrad word processor.

My first sight of a mobile phone must have been at about
the same time. Foolishly, I mocked their early users. Who
could possibly want to know where you'd reached on your
journey home and whether you weren't sure there was any
milk left? And why on earth would one want to ring one's
friend or spouse or mother from the street, anyway? What
possible use were these to anyone, I wondered? Just showing off. My own mobile phone is now so old you can't text
on it (or at least I can't) or take photographs, and I believe
its value, if it has any, is only in its antiquity. It's not just

WikiLeaks and Stieg Larsson's novels that offer us hacking as the new art form. We now live in a world where the young can topple the old because they know something we can only pretend to understand.

May 2011

Reason Not the Need

Peter Mandelson, the Mephistopheles of the Blair and Brown Labour governments, is famous for remarking that he was 'intensely relaxed about people getting filthy rich' so long as they paid their taxes. We are often addressed as 'taxpayers' these days, a tactic allowing us to be simultaneously put-upon victims of scams and frauds, and complicit in manoeuvres to produce and sustain the grossest inequalities. The one-time London boss of a large international bank was recalling on the radio here recently that twenty years ago he earned five times his secretary's salary. The man filling that job now earns more than five hundred times his secretary's salary. A recent survey established that 74 per cent of Britons regard themselves as middle-class and only 26 per cent as working-class (a big drop). No one, apparently, is prepared to describe themselves as upper-class. So has one kind of equality been gained at the expense of another? The difference between the highest earners and owners and the lowest certainly seems greater than it has ever been, though I suppose the owning of great wealth was better hidden in the past, and perhaps money was more discreetly amassed and spent. We all know now that a top-class footballer (not the very best, but one who plays for a top team) expects to earn in a week about six times the average annual UK salary. Such anomalies abound, and have been exacerbated by the recession. We're enjoined to take them in our stride because 'we're all in this together'.

Rummaging through my great-aunt's papers, I found a letter my father had written to her in 1918, when he was twelve years old:

> I have thought out a scheme for people doing without money. People are always to receive enough to keep them vegitating (to vegitate they needn't work); but to have luxuries and live, they must work. The right to have more than just enough to keep body and soul together, is the payment of labour. The value of the certificate varies according to the amount of work performed, and the certificates are used accordingly.

He and the aunt who brought him up admired Alexander Kerensky, who had just been ousted as Prime Minister of Russia. Indeed, his aunt had heard Kerensky lecture in London and wrote to tell her nephew that he had a mouth like a letterbox. She wondered whether the Russian language might require mouths to be that shape.

I am struck by the absence of 'need' in discussion these days of pay and bonuses and liability to taxation. My father grew up to be a pianist rather than an economist. No surprise there. Money, debt, even mortgages, terrified him all his life. But he had grown up knowing something about 'need' and about having more or less than you 'need'. I have just discovered that my Barclays deposit account paid me under 1 per cent interest on the small amount I have sitting there, and that that same sum was taxed at 20 per cent. I can't help wondering what the big boss of Barclays can 'need' all that money *for* (£43 million last year, apparently, in salary and bonuses). We're not allowed to ask. It might look like envy. Does he ever meditate on the discrepancy between his 'need' for all that money and the kinds of 'need' that a majority of the world's population knows about?

Will Hutton, a British writer on economics, was asked a year or so ago by the coalition government to 'investigate the idea of capping senior executive public sector pay at twenty times the lowest-paid person in any public body, but also to examine to what extent such a multiple could become a wider social norm'. He rejected that as an impossible brief (though he doesn't explain why it is impossible, beyond assuring us that it would be 'unfair'). Instead, he has proposed a 'revolution in transparency' and the introduction of fines and penalties as well as bonuses. Hutton's report will no doubt be kicked into the long grass like most such reports, on the grounds that administering his scheme would require a vast monitoring paraphernalia, itself subject to penalties and bonuses of its own.

The Spirit Level, by Richard Wilkinson and Kate Pickett, published in 2009, makes a persuasive case for inequality being even more detrimental to societies than poverty: eroding trust, increasing anxiety and illness, encouraging excessive consumption, and so on. There was a huge march through London some time ago, a mustering of discontents, more than a quarter of a million people, brought together by their anger and doubt about the government's cuts and its dismantling of the welfare state. I hobbled my way to Hyde Park to wave a flag for those forgotten things: equality and need.

June 2011

The Royal We

Joel asked me to write about the royal family, and I imagined he might want a republican diatribe. I was wrong. He emailed me later, 'I am a big proponent of monarchy, since if we are going to live in a celebrity culture, and it seems inescapable, it is more entertaining as the spectator to watch the private lives of people who are famous via a roll of the genetic dice.' The pleasure of writing about things you've never written about before is that you may discover what you think in the process.

The Queen of England (as I think I'm allowed to call her) has had a busy month. She's been to Ireland, a triumphant visit and the first time an English monarch has been there for a hundred years. Colm Tóibín, the novelist, voiced a general satisfaction with this new friendliness, which may also serve to promote the interests of an Ireland mired in debt and difficulty. It's estimated that 100,000 Irish men and women will emigrate this year. Tóibín regards the

Queen as 'dutiful and serious', which she is. Meanwhile, we've been drowning in words like 'historic' and 'symbolism' and that other awful favourite, 'iconic'. Thousands of journalists flocked to Dublin, and many more thousands of policemen. A bomb left in a bus on the outskirts of the city was defused the night before the Queen arrived, so the streets were abruptly emptied of people, and the sounds made by a small crowd of protesters 400 metres away were successfully muffled.

The Queen can usually be counted on to say nothing surprising or inflammatory, though the speech she gave in Dublin (rumoured to contain offerings from a distinguished Irish writer) acknowledged a history of suffering and wrongdoing on both sides. Her husband looked as if he wouldn't mind saying a thing or two, given half a chance. But he wasn't, and is patiently awaiting his ninetieth birthday. Two days later they were back in London welcoming Barack and Michelle Obama. Think of the effort. Changing the bedding in time, dusting the palace for pernickety Americans, getting organic things in for breakfast. Just working out the seating for the banquet apparently took seven hours. I hope the Duke gave her a hand with that. A friend of mine met the Queen many years ago and was impressed by her gentle cognisance – just this side of *Schadenfreude* – of the pickle the United States had got itself into over Vietnam. He thought that despite her sometimes grim demeanour she had a sense of humour.

And she'd already managed that wedding. There were several 'Fuck the Royal Wedding' parties on 29 April, as

well as a lot of the other sort. I was asked to one of the
first kind and was embarrassed when my heart sank at
the thought of missing it all on television. My host had to
cancel his party for quite unroyalist reasons, so I spent a
happy morning watching – without my menfolk – the car-
riages and clothes and hats and bishops, and hearing who'd
been asked and who hadn't. Tony Blair and Gordon Brown
weren't there: a punishment, some say, for outlawing fox
hunting. Sarah Ferguson wasn't there either. Her daughters
made up for it in outlandish style. Five dodgy vols-au-vent,
some wit pointed out, and Princess Beatrice, the older of
the two, could be queen. A survey of people on the day
established that less than half the population of the UK
watched the wedding on television or on the street.

We're all, or nearly all, ambivalent about this peculiar
institution we're saddled with and about the recognisably
and perhaps forgivably dysfunctional family at its centre.
I wish I knew quite why I should want to watch these
strange people at their play and in their hats and uniforms
doing what they do. I don't know them. We've got almost
nothing in common. They spend their days doing things
I've never done, just as I spend mine doing things they've
probably never done. I'm not keen on deference or titles
and sycophancy or servants or hats or blood sports, let
alone Royal Variety Shows or dull military music of the
late nineteenth century, nor, indeed, on godly injunctions
to love, bear fruit, obey, and so on. I was once at a party
to which Princess Margaret had been asked, and was told
that if I encountered her I should curtsy at once and on

no account leave the party until she had. These seemed impossible orders (I was a foot taller than she was, for one thing) and I ducked both, avoiding the curtsy and slinking off before midnight.

I don't want to meet them. I just like wondering about them sometimes, as you might about Elizabeth Bennet or Natasha Rostova. Perhaps they long to escape it all, live like the rest of us, or just wander off as Tsar Alexander I is supposed to have done. I can't imagine a life where one was always on show, there to be admired, perhaps, but also to be excoriated. I couldn't possibly stand still for hours as the Queen does, without wobbling or falling over. I am curious, however, as millions seem to be, as to how these people do it.

July 2011

Welfare

In July 1956, my new young husband, Karl, and I, with two Scottish folksinger friends, Rory and Alexander McEwen, were driving south after a year at Harvard in Massachusetts. We stopped for gas in Alabama and asked the attendant, foolishly no doubt, where we'd find the singers we most admired in New Orleans: Leadbelly and others. 'Oh, we got welfare for that,' he grunted. Bemused, we went on our way. As recent beneficiaries of the new British 'welfare state', we were in favour of 'welfare'. We'd all, if differently, received free university education. Three of us had done two years of National Service, and I would have my first baby a year later on the National Health. Ten years after the end of the Second World War, and we were sure some progress was being made towards greater equality, even some levelling of class difference and division. As it happens, the four of us came from backgrounds that represented pretty well the whole spectrum of class differences in the UK of the day.

I tell this story to illustrate a divergence in the histories of the US and the UK when it comes to thoughts about equality and the different meanings of 'welfare'. The word still holds both of its historical meanings: well-being and charity. I have lived most of my adult life believing that it was the state's business to look after the basic well-being – health, education, pensions, and so on – of all its citizens; and that charitable activity and giving should be directed primarily towards the poor in the rest of the world.

But the welfare state has been unravelling for years in the UK, and the unravelling is speeding up alarmingly at the moment. At last the Right has a persuasive justification for reducing the welfare state to the point of destruction. Cutting public services, we are told, is now essential and virtuous, in order to reduce the 'deficit' caused by the extravagance and laissez-faire of the last government. In their place, we are offered something called the 'Big Society'. No one I know or have read has been able to tell me what this means. When Margaret Thatcher famously declared that there was no such thing as 'society' in the 1980s, there were some Conservatives who winced. So perhaps this is an attempt by her descendants to retrieve the word for themselves, while airily inflating it. The 'Big Society' seems to entail two kinds of change: the willingness of the private sector to step into the gap left by truncated public services and even to find ways to make a profit from them; and a belief that unemployment and poverty will be mitigated mysteriously by some people's willingness to work for nothing. Added to these will be a whole slew of charitable activities performed by self-selected and supposedly benevolent vigilantes.

The New Labour governments of Blair and Brown persisted with Margaret Thatcher's privatising of the railways and the principal utilities and with undermining the unions. They also introduced university fees and private investment into the building and running of schools and hospitals. The result has been that the interest to be repaid on those loans currently forms a large part of the national education and health budgets, and helps to justify precisely those cuts that undermine the welfare state most sharply.

The 1950s can look forlorn from here: food and clothes barely out of rationing, bomb sites in London just starting to be cleared so that new buildings might go up. But things were getting better, opening up. The sixtieth anniversary of the 1951 Festival of Britain is being celebrated this year. I remember it for its enthusiasm and its shabbiness. When I left university four years later I was warned that it would be hard to find work. But suddenly things changed, and we expected to get jobs, earn money, find places to live, though we knew we might not escape the shabbiness.

Five of my six grandchildren are sitting important exams this summer; the oldest is finishing university, the others are teenagers. What will their futures be? It is hard to be encouraging. The cost of university education as well as fierce competition for places makes university a less obvious option than it was for me. And when it comes to jobs, professions, work, they hear only of internships, apprenticeships, and these as only accessible through networking and knowing people. They have to contemplate years of expensive study followed by years of unpaid work. This no longer feels like a country for most young men and women, and it's an uglier place for that.

August 2011

Murdoch and Company

In 2011 the News of the World *was closed down for ever. It was also the year of the London riots. We'd got used to scandals and tales of corruption by then. A number of MPs had already been shown to be fiddling their expenses, and several members of the House of Lords were suspended for the same thing. It may well be that these years will be remembered above all for these scandals and for a public exasperation with politics and politicians, with yellow press journalists and with some high-ranking policemen.*

We're high on Murdoch revelations here, and their repercussions are rushing your way. The trigger was relatively parochial. Someone on the *News of the World* (once the most popular Sunday newspaper in the UK) paid someone else to hack into the phone of a thirteen-year-old girl, Milly Dowler, who disappeared in 2002 and was later found murdered. This was too much; and it brought to a head a long campaign by the *Guardian* newspaper and others to expose endemic hacking in Murdoch's News International and to block his bid to acquire the huge and lucrative chunk of the BSkyB television franchise that he didn't own already.

The story moves so fast that we're reeling. The rest of the press and broadcasting are gorging on it, alluding to a public 'outrage' it's hard to be sure about, glorying in the carefully rehearsed grovelling of the Murdochs, politicians, police officers, journalists, all implicated in newfangled as well as old-as-the-hills corruption. The *News of the World* is gone after 168 years. The BSkyB bid has been withdrawn. Two top dogs of London's police force have had to resign, both angrily implying that the Mayor of London, Boris Johnson, and the Prime Minister, David Cameron, wanted them out to save their own bacon.

We are settling down here for an afternoon's theatre on television. Murdoch himself, Rebekah Brooks, his 'flame-haired' acolyte and quasi daughter at the centre of the story, and Murdoch's son James will be publicly interrogated by a parliamentary committee. We anticipate an operatic tableau rather than more spilled beans. Lawyers on all sides will be anxious that nothing gets in the way of future criminal proceedings. And Rebekah and Andy Coulson – her predecessor as editor of the *News of the World*, who had to resign as the Prime Minister's press officer – have both been arrested and let out on bail.* Rebekah was married at one point to an actor who played a particularly

---

* Rebekah Brooks was acquitted of all charges against her and is now back working at News UK.

unsavoury East End thug and crook in a television soap. He was once very publicly felled to the ground by his wife. Rebekah apparently goes riding (hacking, indeed) at weekends with the Prime Minister. These facts have not helped her. It took her ten days to resign, and it has been said by rival journalists that she can't have been much of an editor, since she rejected the offer of the MPs' expenses scoop on the grounds that there was no sex in it.

The *Independent* estimates that there are 10,000 private investigators in the UK, some of them holding college diplomas in hacking and bugging. Rupert Murdoch has published apologies in most of the other newspapers, conceding that things at the *News of the World*, if not elsewhere in his empire, had got out of hand. The original whistleblower there, Sean Hoare, was found dead, probably from drugs and drink. He maintained that hacking was not just widespread across much of the British press, but at News International you could get the sack for *not* hacking when you were asked to. Many, including Nick Davies of the *Guardian*, believed him.

The rest of the press has, by and large, wallowed in the belief that public opinion is appalled above all by the hacking of vulnerable people as well as celebrities. But most of us have assumed for some time that such things went on. We may be angrier about the kowtowing of intimidated politicians to Murdoch and his mafia, by their malign influence on this government and the last, and by growing evidence of police corruption and involvement in underhand journalistic activities and, even more, in their cover-up. The police had enough evidence to charge News International with these crimes two years ago, but they didn't open the plastic bags that contained the evidence. And there's not much doubt that Murdoch influenced Blair's decision to fall in with Bush and take us into the Iraq war. His pressure to keep us in a permanently ambiguous relation to Europe, and his rather successful attempts to clip the wings of the BBC, have been resented for a long time.

We have had more than a decade of seriously dodgy public life, starting from the government's lying about WMDs in Iraq, their encouragement of the banks' unregulated and risky dealings, along with the MPs' fiddling of expenses. Gordon Brown has been more or less silent since he ceased to be Prime Minister over a year ago, but last week was a roaring Job in the House of Commons, blaming his most senior adviser for advising him not to investigate Murdoch just before the general election. He had nothing to say about why he took the advice he so disapproved of.

Asked recently whether he reads the *Guardian* newspaper, the Duke of Edinburgh replied 'No fear'. We are partisan and snobbish about newspapers in this country. I'd have the Duke down as a *Telegraph* man, whereas I'm all too obviously, I'm afraid, a *Guardian* woman, who has seldom read the *News of the World*. An eighty-year-old woman recently related how her mother would primly explain that, of course, she did not read it for the dirt. 'But,' she added, 'you have to know about these things.' And wouldn't that paper have relished the pace, the drama, the sheer rush and explosion of news, and our expectation that there is more, much more to come? We wake to new arrests, resignations, apologies, volte-faces. We discuss each speech for hidden meanings, accusations, hints about what we may still be told.

There's a temptation to wonder whether the world was always as corrupt as it has seemed during the years of this new century. Perhaps its dirty deeds were done more decorously. A permanent theatre of exposure, of public inquiries and commissions into the lies of bankers and politicians and newspapers owners and football managers has not encouraged trust or confidence in the powerful.

We're assured that this could inspire a healthy cleaning up, that we'll be better for it in the end, that we'll learn lessons from it and see that 'it never happens again'. Ed Miliband, who has wilted a bit as leader of the Labour Party, is now St George, well into his stride, as he dissociates himself from the Blair/Brown sycophancies and hails the prospect of a dismantled Murdoch empire. That now looks likely enough to occasion one or two expressions of pity for Rupert, an ailing old fox, no longer fit to protect himself or his young and wondering whether he is to be hunted down in the USA. He assured the committee interrogating him today that it was 'the most humble day of my life'. He had his wife to thank for the swift deflection of an ugly attack by an indignant intruder.

September 2011

Bad Language

I recently published a scholarly pair of articles (not by me) on how English has changed over the centuries and how teachers might make use of these changes. My Editorial for that issue of the quarterly journal I edit, appropriately called *Changing English*, began with a heartfelt declaration 'that the English language has a long history, that it has thrived on change and has resisted the fixed, the conventional and the anodyne with a wonderfully sturdy capacity to renew itself'. I grew up with a father possessed of strong views about pronunciation and other linguistic matters, which he did not keep to himself. I've prided myself on standing out against a good deal of all that and of encouraging linguistic laissez-faire in the young. When I taught English years ago I would often be asked whether it was all right to use 'language', which meant 'bad language'. 'Go ahead,' I'd say, 'so long as there's some point to it.'

The truth is, however, that I'm as squeamish as anyone

else when it comes to some recent novelties. Can't you see what the problem is, I want occasionally and shame-facedly to ask, with 'unacceptable' and 'bottom line' and 'at the end of the day'? And why has 'mouth-watering' suddenly become 'eye-watering'?

In England, objections to other people's language tend to start from class, educational and then regional differences and could be said to travel in more than one direction. 'Posh' language, 'la-di-da' speech that sounds too like written language, is mocked, just as dropped aitches and confusions about 'I' and 'me' may be. In her marvellous book on the subject, *Verbal Hygiene*, Deborah Cameron, the Oxford linguist, writes about an upper-class woman emerging from a spell in prison to insist that the worst thing about it was other prisoners 'mangling the English language'. As Cameron writes,

> She wanted her audience to believe that she had borne without complaint the loss of her liberty, the humiliation of being labelled a common criminal, the lack of privacy and of luxury, the separation from loved ones; but that having to hear the other women's glottal stops and split infinitives . . . had driven her to distraction.

Even my father would not have gone as far as that, despite his tortured dismay at the pass things had come to.

I'm not sure that my sudden explosions of linguistic disapproval really are provoked by class or education, and I am learning to accept that 'hopefully' and 'disinterested' mean something different now and that their old meanings may be beyond rescue, even if, as with 'disinterested', its replacements – 'unbiased', 'unprejudiced', 'impartial', for instance – can't quite stand in for it. What I mind more are those formulaic phrases drummed up by politicians and flaunted by journalists as ways of deflecting our questions, reassuring us when we shouldn't be reassured, cutting off argument. Some are meant to suggest conviction, which is apparently always a good thing, admirable, always persua-sive, even when it's obviously misplaced. We've had prime ministers recently 'passionately believing' things, and entirely sure that something is 'the right thing to do' and 'the right thing for our country'. These are weasel words, which bypass the expectation that we might be told exactly why we have gone to war, why the National Health Service will be even better once it has been privatised and reduced, why bankers must be indulged and everyone else must take it on the chin, and so on.

This is odd at a time when we're also, just as rhetorically and vapidly, asked for our opinions about everything. The BBC constantly asks us to send in our thoughts on this and that. Somewhere there must be an enormous and proba-bly virtual bin, into which our emails and texts, ritually ignored, are shredded and disposed of.

Then there are the new phrases for 'reforms' that have suddenly and inexplicably become essential. Perfectly workable institutions are described as 'not fit for purpose', usually in order to save money. There are the constant injunctions to ignore what has gone wrong, forget who caused the trouble, and 'draw a line under it', 'move on', focus on 'going forward'. And then there is the new use of 'humble': winners of prizes describe themselves as feeling 'humble' or even 'humbled', when what they mean is that they feel particularly pleased with themselves, embarrassingly so, and why shouldn't they?

Perhaps this is just contemporary political and media jargon, no more obfuscating than it ever was. And perhaps it is simply that language changes too fast for us, and we stick to the clichés and formulae of our youth. The curious thing is that the inventions of the young, the abbreviations, the new meanings for 'hot', 'cool', 'chill', 'buff', 'fit', 'lame', seem alive and promising in comparison, derived from their own quite different experience of literacy and communication. I've heard, for instance, that those texters and Internet fiends in Cairo's Tahrir Square and other parts of the Middle East have developed ways of writing colloquial, spoken forms of Arabic which not only express their new meanings, but, unlike classical written Arabic, allow them to represent their linguistic differences from one another. I shall remember that next time I find myself wincing at some unbearable neologism.

October 2011

School Choice and the Feral Underclass

As of March 2015, 400 'free' schools have been approved and 500 more were promised by the Conservatives if they were to win the next general election. The most obvious objections are that such schools are not started in areas where there is a serious shortage of places, that they eat into the stability and funding of other local schools, and that they are ready to employ unqualified teachers.

England has 'a feral underclass'. So says Ken Clarke, the Justice Secretary, thought by some to be the least inhumane (or do I mean inhuman?) member of the coalition government. Tony Blair, our one-time Prime Minister, has reprimanded David Cameron, the current one, for talking about 'pockets of society that are not only broken, but frankly sick' and insisted that there are only a few hundred thousand or so 'outside the social mainstream'.

He meant that most of us are fine, yet whole families are cast as literally beyond the pale, or as Clarke put it, 'cut off from the mainstream in everything but its materialism'. He might have substituted 'material'. All the riots this summer began in areas of high poverty and unemployment. Mentioning that nowadays invites accusations of 'apology'.

Some rioters' families are to have welfare and housing benefits withdrawn. Unusually long prison sentences are all very well, but three out of five rioters already had previous convictions, and our prisons are overflowing. Now looters and arsonists, several to a cell, are inconveniently filling up space that might otherwise be inhabited by decent bankers and journalists and MPs, who have fiddled their expenses and are entitled to some privacy in this, their hour of need.

Who's to blame? Well, parents, of course. But schools too. The language, like the reactions, has become at once savage and ineffectual. All this coincides with an excellent new book called *School Wars*, by Melissa Benn, daughter of Tony Benn, one of the few radical politicians to survive into the twenty-first century. Her book tells the story of the self-sabotage and 'conservative vandalism', that have dogged our education system since its beginnings after the Second World War. This system is now crumbling beneath a multitude of schemes designed to effect the 'state-subsidised privatisation' of schools, a process meant to bypass local authorities and to rid schools of the contamination of democratic accountability and control.

So-called 'free' schools may employ unqualified teachers (no more nonsense about subject knowledge or under-standing how children learn), pay them what they choose (independently of national pay deals), expel children who give them any trouble, develop their own admissions cri-teria and procedures, and if possible make a profit out of it.

Twenty-four 'free' schools were hurriedly opened in the autumn of 2011, barely a year after they were first pro-posed. They are modelled on American Charter Schools and Swedish free schools. The first of these secondary schools has just opened in my part of London, draining an immediate £15 million from the three other secondary schools in the district, which are each due to lose £20 million from government cuts. The new school caters for 120 blazered children, for whom Latin is compulsory until fourteen, and History (British) to sixteen.

England (and in this respect it is worse than Scotland, Wales or Northern Ireland) has the most unequal, unfair and most segregated education system in Europe. These developments will make things worse. A majority of par-ents and teachers, when asked, want local, co-educational, mixed-ability schools, what we used to call 'comprehen-sives'. But they aren't asked. Instead, they're told they have 'choice'; though in fact it is schools that choose children, and only the very rich or the very lucky get to choose schools. Parents are also offered 'diversity'. Schools that we all pay for can refuse children of the wrong gender, the wrong religion, the wrong parents, the wrong grades at eleven. If your child goes to a school you don't want her to go to you're hardly likely to be overjoyed by the presence of a new Sikh free school down the road for which your child is ineligible, or by another school nearby which is to be staffed by men (and perhaps women) recently sacked from the military, due to cuts. Two birds with one stone, I suppose.

Governments have always approved of parents who don't want their children mixing with riff-raff; and they've done their best to see that the children of the 'feral underclass' remain that way, by leaving them in schools so starved of resources that other parents will move heaven and earth to send their children elsewhere.

It hardly takes the forty years or so I've spent teaching children and teachers in this country's state system to know that telling children they are failures is likely to discourage them from giving their full attention to learning and doing well at school. Nor does telling them that they have rotten parents, who should go to parenting classes, engender respect for authority. Tony Blair regarded the move towards a genuinely comprehensive school system as 'pretty close to academic vandalism'. Melissa Benn imagines what such a service might be like, were it allowed to exist:

A service that allows the poorest family to feel confident that their child will receive a broadly similar educational start in life to their better-off peers, and one that promises to enrich and challenge all. A service based on neighbourhood schools – housed in well-designed, well-equipped, aesthetically pleasing and properly maintained buildings, enjoying plenty of outdoor space – with balanced intakes and a broad, rich curriculum that will allow each child, whatever their talents, temperament or interests, to flourish.

Vandalism? It sounds more like utopia to me.

November 2011

Dickens and Money

I've been reading Claire Tomalin's new biography of Charles Dickens. It's been the first and is probably the best of several books published to celebrate the bicentenary of his birth at the beginning of 2012. Money mattered to Dickens, the having of it and the lack of it. His father was imprisoned for debt, and family indigence meant that Dickens received little formal education and even spent a year as a very young boy working for six shillings a week in a blacking factory. His beginnings as a jobbing journalist rapidly turned him into an extraordinarily successful writer, and by the end of his life he wrote of needing £9,000 a year to support his ten children, his discarded wife, his mistress and her family. That would be about £630,000 by today's standards: not quite what bankers expect, and less than the head of the BBC and most top-level footballers.

Dickens never forgave America for pirating his books

and paying him nothing for their copyright, and he responded by going on punishing reading tours from which he made the equivalent of £1.4 million. His final tour probably killed him; he died of a cerebral haemorrhage at fifty-eight, not long after returning from America to his home in Kent.

His novels are full of money, real and virtual. He was, as we all are, bewildered by the absence of the stuff for most of the time, and his characters can seem relieved to be

dealing with actual coins – even when there are very few of them – that can be exchanged for real things: a loaf, a bed, a jacket, a waistcoat. How can we not be suspicious of 'that mysterious paper currency which circulates in London when the wind blows, gyrated here and there and everywhere . . . caught by the electric wires'? 'Paper money' put the fear of God into the contemporaries of Dickens and Walter Scott in that great age of bankruptcy.

Dickens's novels are haunted by the vanishing of actual money into its ghostly stand-ins. Will we go on trusting banks to hold on to it for us when we barely see the real stuff? Years and whole lives are wasted contesting wills and their promise of fortunes in *Bleak House*, and at the end there is nothing. Blown away. Mr Boffin, the Golden Dustman of *Our Mutual Friend*, presides over his lucrative rubbish dumps, 'a prey to prosperity' as Dickens puts it, but 'a pretty fair scholar in dust' in his own eyes.

What would Dickens have made of the Bank of England's £75 billion worth of 'quantitative easing', the printing of notes (or not even that) to be exchanged for bonds as fictitious as they are? Could someone have helped Mr Micawber to 'restructure' his debt? The idea of electronic money, as it has been called, would have appealed to Dickens, who seems to have had faith in spontaneous combustion and to have practised mesmerism. And the Circumlocution Office in *Little Dorrit*, its purpose to confuse and trip up the foolish and the unfortunate. It's still there. Poor debtors that we are, struggling to discover how to spend and save at the same time, as we're enjoined to. So poor Mr Dorrit struggles with the world of finance that hobbles and bamboozles him with words:

> The affairs of this debtor were perplexed by a partnership, of which he knew no more than that he had invested money in it; by which legal matters of assignment and settlement, conveyance here and conveyance there, suspicion of unlawful preference of creditors in this direction, and of mysterious spiriting away of property in that; and as nobody on the face of the earth could be more incapable of explaining any single item in the heap of confusion than the debtor himself, nothing comprehensible could be made of his case.

I don't find myself imagining Mrs Merkel's euros packaged and shipped in galleons manned by galley slaves as they make their way to Piraeus and Athens and thence in saddlebags to the islands and mountain villages of Greece. Nor do I envisage those billions of spanking new fifty-pound notes in their wads and elastic bands dumped on the doorsteps of the small-business owners so often invoked as needier than any of us, and on whom we are said to rely. But I would like someone to explain why, if the Bank of England can create billions of new money, that isn't the answer for other countries. Why not Greece too? Since these billions and trillions of dollars and pounds and yen are all virtual and appear to represent nothing concrete in the real world, why can't we simply create as much as we need? And why does 'default' mean opposite things? Home base, level playing field, as well as debt and Mr Micawber's 'misery'. And what happens in a 'bailout'? There's a new term too: 'haircut', which I take to mean some sort of trimming or, perhaps, rake-off. Dickens would have enjoyed that, I think.

I have a young relation who describes himself as an anarchist and would like to see the end of states and the end of money. He may by the sheerest good luck live to see his wishes fulfilled. If money doesn't disappear altogether it seems certain that we're all going to see a great deal less of it.

December 2011

Occupy

Four years later and it's hard to remember the sweetness and hope of Occupy, the pleasure of London sharing its politics with New York, the confidence I had in my young guide and his sense of a movement he might applaud and even join. Seen from the ellipses and the rough-hewn arguments of the 2015 general election and since, this particular protest gleams and wilts simultaneously.

Paternoster Square, at the heart of the City of London, is the grim and newish development owned by Mitsubishi. In addition it contains the London Stock Exchange, Goldman Sachs, Merrill Lynch and a number of bars and restaurants which offer themselves as glamorous and expensive. It was there that the Occupy protesters planned to set up their tents, but the police stepped in, and this ugly and unloved spot is now guarded and impenetrable by the public. The tents were moved round the corner to the forecourt of St Paul's Cathedral; and if there are a few who feel that the squabbles behind those vast ecclesiastical doors have distracted from the protest itself, there are many who are grateful for them.

Two senior clerics – one a well-known broadcaster, Giles Fraser – felt obliged to resign, apparently for supporting the protesters outside. The Archbishop of Canterbury wrote an article in the *Financial Times* supporting the protesters and arguing for a 'Robin Hood Tax' on financial transactions, a move proposed by Angela Merkel and rejected summarily by David Cameron. The good behaviour of the protesters, their tidiness, their ecumenical stance and their leaderless-ness, have been given a warmer welcome here than anyone expected, perhaps as a consequence of those ecclesiastical distractions.

Much of the discussion has focused on charges that the church is divided and hypocritical when it comes to sup-porting the 99 per cent against the 1 per cent, who do a good deal of their business a whisker away from our princi-pal cathedral, which could be said, in its turn, to join in all that money-making with alacrity by charging nearly £15 for an adult wishing to visit it. On the day I went to the site, the tents huddled somewhat, though they were arranged in about twenty neat rows of ten. They had moved by then from the forecourt to a less showy pavement at one side of St Paul's. In their midst was a line of recycling bins and a quartet of toilets. There was a book tent and a university tent, in which two young men, a Jew and a Muslim, were engaged in heated, non-violent exchange. Tents these days require no pegs of the kind I remember hammering with difficulty into the ground. They are light bubbles of brightly coloured nylon that look as though they might easily take off like kites in a strong wind.

I was there for the General Assembly after lunch, a mild and friendly occasion, at which anyone might have their say and those with technical skills were encouraged to offer their services at the Information Tent. That was a surprise, since such skills are assumed to flourish among protesters these days, especially if they're young. But then some of these protesters are almost as old as I am. An emissary from Wall Street, adorned with an ill-fitting dog collar intended to honour the venue, perhaps, and a shock of preternaturally white hair, brought greetings from the Big Apple. A charming woman offered a poster that could be adapted and distributed by protesters of quite different persuasions. Famous visitors, proudly invoked, have included Tony Benn, Caroline Lucas, our only Green MP, and Julian Assange. Christians, Muslims and Jews announce their presence with handwritten posters above their tents and on the surrounding pillars.

My stern young guide approved as I did of this gathering of differences and of the absence of the big political parties. Some of the protesters are people made homeless by repossessions, which now happen, I'm told, at a rate of one every twenty-five minutes. My guide also approved of the slowness of it all, of the acceptance that revolution, infinitely desirable, is hardly imminent, though he is determined to devote his own life to ending all stock exchanges, corporations and banks. The Occupy movement draws him as it draws many here of all ages. We are impressed that it is a quietly spreading international movement, mostly of the young, and that its focus is on inequality and unfairness.

More than a week later, and the camp has survived the dismantling of the New York Zuccotti Park camp and threats that the police plan to move them from their St Paul's site at dusk. Their lawyers have managed to delay things. The original camp has sprung new versions of itself, in Finsbury Square and in a huge empty building in Hackney, east London, property of the Swiss UBS bank. To everyone's surprise, including that of the protesters themselves, I suspect, the London Occupy movement is a success. It has created new alliances and articulated a new kind of activism. Expectations of mockery, violence, more riots, have been frustrated. Twenty bishops (two of them arch), provoked by public criticism, have declared their opposition to the coalition's benefit cuts. The movement may be thought small and quiet, or too broad and indeterminate in its aims, but it is gathering support and enthusiasm for its breadth and for its exasperation with banks and big business and with a coalition government that nobody voted for. More people are moved by inequality and injustice than any of our three main political parties seem to have thought possible. There is to be a national strike before long. It will be interesting to see what has been learned, if anything, from the Occupy movement.

January 2012

Austerity

I've always liked the words austerity and austere: they suggest simplicity, things that have been intelligently and properly pared down, shorn of distraction and unnecessary ornament. Now they're words forever associated with meanness, inequality, a state of affairs imposed by the rich on the poor as both a virtue and a challenge. Anyone who objects to the politics of austerity may be charged with encouraging the politics of envy.

No more boom and bust, said Gordon Brown, Chancellor of the Exchequer in 1997, New Labour's first year in government. Now we are reminded daily that we are experiencing an era of austerity and that things will get worse. We must all (or perhaps not quite all) tighten our belts. This may be less of a shock for those of us who remember Britain during the 1930s and the Second World War. We tell ourselves that we managed then without cars or washing machines or refrigerators. We grew quite fond of our ration books and gave a lot of thought to what could be bought with our clothing coupons. We didn't get scurvy or get fat on a diet without oranges and bananas. Indeed, it is generally thought that the British people benefited from a more balanced and nutritious diet during the war than they'd had before it. One egg a week and two ounces of butter doesn't sound much. But the rations were subsidised, and plenty of people couldn't have afforded butter at all before the war.

There was something levelling about those war years, despite films and novels that revel in the antics of the servanted classes, freezing in their unheated castles. Houses certainly were very cold in those days. Few of them had central heating. The pop-popping of gas fires, and the violent heat of electric ones you had practically to sit on, accompany all my memories of reading, curled up

on the floor and trying to keep warm. And most people rented their homes in those days rather than owning them. Renting and not owning is seen nowadays as a misfortune, emblematic of the times, almost the denial of a human right, though it is also coming back into fashion.

A return to some of those lacks and scarcities would be hard for my generation, but harder still for the next one, let alone the one after that. By the middle of the 1950s we were pretty certain that life was getting better and that it would go on doing so. And it did. Our parents expected their children to have an easier time of it than they had had. Now most parents worry that their children will have far more to contend with than they did. I suppose the best we can hope for is that life for most people doesn't sharply deteriorate.

So far, it is undoubtedly the young who come off worst. And that really is a change. Youth unemployment is higher than it's been since 1992, and though employment among graduates has risen a little from its recent nadir, it is not much more than 80 per cent. There are more than half a million unemployed young people between the ages of sixteen and twenty-four – NEETs, they're called: 'Not in Education, Employment or Training' – many of whom have been looking for work for a year or more.

On the face of it, the government is warier of cutting services for the old than for the young; we vote, and the young do so less. Even so, there have been disturbing revelations. The bankruptcy of the largest private supplier of old-age care homes is one. There are tales of cruelty and neglect of old people in care homes and hospitals, and the possibility that the old constantly find themselves at the back of the queue waiting for medical attention. The moderately serious suggestion that old people should be required to downsize their homes in order to release spare bedrooms for the homeless has been another suggestion. We may need any spare bedrooms we have for friends, carers and homeless grandchildren. Public sector workers are having to pay more for pensions that will be smaller than ours and delivered at a later date. Many people will be happy to go on working, but many won't. And no thought has been given to what happens when the young are blocked from work which is still being performed by people in their sixties or even seventies.

It's possible to feel that the worst effects of recession are a new callousness, a new set of rationales for inequality. Apparently a majority of us blames the poor for their situation and despises them for wanting all the material things that the richer and the rich take for granted. Ruthlessness and competitiveness prevail and are admired. Dishonesty surprises and shocks us hardly at all. The government blames Europe, the last Labour government and the reckless, improvident poor for all our ills, and a majority of those who are asked for their opinion seem to agree with them. Even the fact that a million people make use of food banks is greeted with disbelief rather than horror.

Yet I have Irish friends who are scathing about reports in English newspapers that they are suffering appalling hardship. My friends believe we're far too sorry for ourselves and too patronising about them. It's all nonsense, they say.

The Irish are used to austerity and as their boom time only lasted for about ten years and didn't fool anyone they feel up to the austerity they're required to go back to.

I am torn between pessimism about the effects of new levels of poverty on this unequal society and optimism about the vitality and generosity of Occupy and other signs of new political engagement that take austerity as given.

February 2012

The Iron Lady

Meryl Streep impersonates Margaret Thatcher wonderfully in *The Iron Lady*. A good deal of the film has Thatcher in her dressing gown, mildly demented and remembering or misremembering her middle years, when, from 1979 to 1990, she was Conservative Prime Minister of Britain, the first and only woman in the job, which she occupied for longer than anyone else in the twentieth century. She was much liked and much disliked, and she still is. While the film settles for comedy rather than excoriation, the discomfort one feels watching Thatcher going mad and being mad is mitigated by the suggested possibility that she was never entirely sane. Her 'I will not go mad' echoes King Lear while also calling into question her right to imagine herself in such grandly tragic company.

Someone else plays the young Thatcher, who adores her father, despises her mother and marries a kindly duffer she comes to rely on. By the time she is, extraordinarily enough, leading the Tory Party, she and Meryl Streep are one. Laughed at by her almost solidly male and snobbish party colleagues as the shrill daughter of a provincial grocer, she becomes their leader, providing them with exactly the homilies her father had offered her; and the scenes where these grey-suited men do her bidding like small boys hoping to please Nanny, and not altogether averse to her smacks, are amongst the funniest in the film.

What are sometimes called the 'Thatcher Years' are not by and large remembered warmly, nor were they funny. Ian Gilmour, an old-style patrician Tory (one of her so-called 'wets'), whom Thatcher sacked from her first government in 1981, wrote of the 'devastation' caused by her fervent adoption of Friedmanite monetarist policies. His book, *Dancing with Dogma*, which came out two years after the end of her reign, records some achievements, but reminds us that child poverty doubled during those years, that the tax burden shifted from the rich to the poor, where it has remained, and that 'British society became coarser and more selfish. Attitudes were encouraged which would even have undermined the well-being of a much more prosperous society'. Britain became, Gilmour believed, 'probably the most right-wing state in Western Europe'. If that is the verdict of a high Tory, imagine the feelings she inspired in many of the rest of us.

Thatcher pronounced herself from the beginning a 'conviction' politician who had absolutely no time for consensus, and this was Gilmour's principal objection to her. Agreement, he wrote, 'effectively meant a one-woman consensus, a state of affairs which rendered debate superfluous'. Tony Blair, the Labour Prime

Minister from 1997 to 2007, never hid his admiration for her, and it was from her that he learned the language that denies debate: 'I passionately believe that . . . ', indeed, 'I only know what I believe', and 'It is the right thing to do' have come to be offered ever since as rationale or clinching argument. The last thirty years have seen a damaging diminution in parliamentary and cabinet debate in Britain.

The film has provoked a great deal of journalistic response. There have been surprising claims for Thatcher as a proto-feminist, as an inspiration to later generations of young women, for whom the sky is now the limit. One Sunday paper suggested that there is currently a clutch of right-wing feminists in parliament, which I hope is a contradiction in terms. And there has certainly been a move among some women who describe them-selves as feminist to insist that there is no inconsistency in women pursuing their ambitions just as she did, while concerning themselves not at all with other women or, indeed, with whether particular policies affect women for good or ill. Femininity is seen in the film as an una-voidable fate, which can at times be turned to a woman's advantage, and that was probably Thatcher's view of the matter. Her promise to herself that she at least would never waste time washing teacups as her mother had done – 'one's life must mean more than that' – is echoed in the last scene of the film, where that is exactly what she is doing as the credits come up. The woman who believed that 'there is no such thing as society' ends her film life alone and outside the world she influenced so disastrously, against a soundtrack that tellingly mingles the ghostly cheers of the multitude with her own equally ghostly sighs.

March 2012

Courage

I'm impressed by bravery, of course, but I can't help feeling sorry for villains who get caught and for cowards and their families. It's not that I identify with villains, but I do identify with people who are caught out. Poor Captain Schettino has been jailed for sixteen years for the manslaughter of thirty-two people; deservedly, I suppose. But I fear I'd have done no better. Some of those brave young men I wrote about at the time, who were fighting in Libya and in Syria in 2012, have died or even, in some cases, changed sides. As I write nearly four years later, the newspapers have been full of the beheadings carried out by 'Jihadi John', or Mohammed Emwazi, who was once a sweet-faced pupil at a school in North London I used to visit to work with student teachers who might easily have taught him. Failure, ignominy, villainy are, unfortunately, more interesting than their opposites.

I suppose most of us live with some kind of anxiety that in a fire, a shipwreck, an earthquake or a battle, we'd save our skins, run for our lives and ignore the plight of everyone else.

We jeer, surely uneasily, at J. Bruce Ismay, the owner of the *Titanic*, who leapt into a lifeboat when a thousand 'gentlemen simply stood about the decks, smoking cigarettes, talking to one another, and waiting for the hour to strike', as Frances Wilson records in her book, *How to Survive the Titanic*. For Ismay as for Joseph Conrad's Lord Jim, what happened to him was a matter of chance, there to be snatched at or missed. Ismay spent the rest of his life explaining what had happened, to the world and to himself, managing his guilt, but eternally dishonoured. Lord Jim's jump deprives him decisively of the heroic life he'd hoped and imagined for himself, a shadowy dream that remains with him for ever.

Captain Francesco Schettino, who seems to have been responsible for running the *Costa Concordia* aground off the coast of Tuscany in January 2012 and for swiftly fleeing the scene, having, it is said, 'slipped and fallen into a lifeboat', is despised and vilified in Italy and elsewhere for his cowardice as well as his good looks and his permatan.

Some of my discomfort may be due to the 'women and children first' aspect of it all, and to that other tradition, which has women brandishing the white feather in the face of pacifists and conscientious objectors. It's all too easy to imagine one's own cowardice, fear, reliance on women being let off first and freed from reproach. What is much more difficult to imagine is the extraordinary bravery of, for instance, those young, barely trained and lightly armed Libyans who faced up to a professional army and its tanks in Misrata. And the Egyptians, the young men and women in Tahrir Square, confronted by baton-wielding policemen.

It's not just a question of whether or not one would do the right thing in an emergency, it's about whether those of us who fulminate about injustice and cruelty at home or in other parts of the world would really risk our own lives for our beliefs and whether we rely too easily on the willingness of other people, particularly the young, to fling themselves into the most terrifying dangers.

Was it anger, frustration, despair or camaraderie that led those Syrians in Homs to pit themselves against the crack units of a modern army that has been simply mowing them down? When is courage foolhardiness, and when is it wrong? Can you be brave and foolish or even wicked at the same time? What are we to think about suicide bombers, those young men, for example, who in 2005 killed themselves in London along with more than fifty other people, randomly targeted, and seriously wounded double that number? Weren't they impossibly brave too? Or do you have to fight to be brave? Those bombers had families and lives to live and were prepared to sacrifice themselves for an idea, a hope, a vision, a version of their religion, however distorted. What moved them? And what do we make of that readiness to die for a cause when we disapprove of the cause? All that most of us can say is that we wouldn't risk our lives for those things.

There was, on a mantelpiece in my parents' house and on those of some of my aunts and uncles, a small framed photograph of an intense young man with clenched fists. He was John Cornford, someone they'd all known, though he was younger than they were, who'd died in Spain in 1936,

when he was twenty-one, having gone there to fight on the Republican side. He was always referred to as a Communist and a poet, and was remembered as awkward, obstinate, impatient; and though he was so young he'd had more than one love affair and had fathered a son. I never knew him, though I later came to know that son, who is dead now, but was about my age. The determined young face of his father, and the ubiquity of that photograph, remain with me, and I can't help wondering whether my parents and many of their generation were haunted, and perhaps even shamed, by the courage he'd shown in rushing to Spain; courage that was sometimes deplored and thought foolish.

April 2012

Larissa

Since I wrote this, Larissa and her family have become British citizens, and Larissa has passed her driving test. However, they live with the greatest anxiety about Larissa's brother back in the Ukraine. He and his family have been bombed out of their Donetsk flat and have moved westwards. He and his wife are well into their sixties, and he is ill with a heart condition, waiting for an operation. They get no pensions, and most of the time they live without electricity or running water. In so far as they are engaged politically in the current war in Ukraine it is as opponents of the Kiev government, which they think is in thrall to oligarchs and fascists. Their adopted daughter is currently in London, staying with Larissa and her family and hoping against hope that she'll be allowed to stay here. I write about her plight in 'Peace and War' (p.189).

I've just finished reading *Life and Fate*, Vasily Grossman's vast novel about life in the Soviet Union in the early 1940s;

a book he never saw published. Its central event is the battle of Stalingrad, which looms over the novel as Austerlitz does over Tolstoy's *War and Peace*. Grossman's hero reminds himself that 'for a thousand years Russia had been governed by an absolute autocracy, by Tsars and their favourites. But never had anyone held such power as Stalin.' This is the week when Putin returns, ostensibly elected, as President of Russia, and heir to a new version of absolute power. He was born the year before Stalin's death in 1953, and my friend Larissa was born a year later: both of them right in the middle of what the Russian poet Mandelstam called 'the wolfhound century'.

Larissa was born in Siberia, in Chita, where her grandfather, one of Stalin's hated 'kulaks', had moved his family from the collective farm he'd been forced into and out of in the 1930s. When her parents were divorced – Larissa was about nine – her mother took her and her two older siblings first to her sister in the Kursk district and then to the Ukrainian steel-producing city of Donetsk. These are enormous distances and unimaginably different places. Larissa remembers Siberia with affection and has nothing but hatred for Donetsk, where she and Sasha, the man she married, worked for over twenty years as experienced and qualified engineers for the Russian railways and the military. As Russians, Larissa tells me, they never felt entirely at home in the Ukraine, and things got much worse once Ukraine became independent.

By 1998, life had become so difficult that they decided to come to London. Sasha, Larissa's husband, came first, and she followed him some months later. They came as 'Asylum Seekers', a depressingly supplicant label, which left them living with the sort of uncertainty they had grown up with and knew all too well. A 'mistake', eventually admitted to by the Home Office, put Sasha in prison for four months, while he resisted deportation, went on hunger strike and Larissa found a lawyer who got him out. Miraculously, they seem to have forgiven this 'mistake', remembering perhaps that it was impossible to get anyone released from a Soviet

jail. They both found work, infinitely beneath their capabilities and experience, but they are hard workers and they have done well. They own the house they live in with their daughter, their son-in-law and two small grandsons, and were saved again from possible deportation by the presence of their son-in-law, who, as a Spaniard, is a citizen of the European Union, and therefore entitled to live here permanently with his extended family. Larissa's son and his family prosper in Canada, meanwhile. The London family are all applying for British citizenship.

Once a week for the last ten years, Larissa has crossed London to come to my house, where we read Russian together. We've read Chekhov stories and a lot of Turgenev and Pushkin (Larissa can recite dozens of verses from *Eugene Onegin*), and we're reading Tolstoy's *Resurrection* now, a novel that lambasts Russian officialdom, the law, and the treatment of dissidents and miscreants, with even greater fervour than Grossman. I read a page in Russian, and Larissa reads the next one in English. We're both trying to get better at the other one's language. Larissa also cleans our floors and irons our shirts. She would much rather be doing the work she was trained to do, but she performs these tasks with the energy and the intelligence she gives to everything in her life.

My father taught himself Russian in the war, with a little help from one of the few Russian people we knew, a very old lady who'd been washed on to British shores in the 1930s and knew everything there was to know about mushrooms. I learned some Russian later. And though I've paid one brief visit to Moscow, neither my father nor I imagined that we would ever visit Russia or talk to real Russians. We were satisfied with reading Russian books.

There are officially about 35,000 Russians living in Britain now, and I guess that number might be multiplied by ten if it included people who are not here legally or who were seen as Russians in Soviet times – Latvians, say, or Moldovans. There are, of course, the oligarchs, but there are also Russians like Sasha and Larissa, who are managing to make a life here. There is something marvellous to me that I should now be able to talk bad Russian and read Russian novels and poems with this wise and rosy Russian woman, who has lived through nearly sixty turbulent and battering years to honour us now with her charm and her optimism.

May 2012

Mothers

Nearly thirty years ago I was trying to write a book about women novelists and the men in their books. Partly inspired by Adrienne Rich, the poet and essayist who died a year or two ago, and her *Of Woman Born*, I began with a memory:

> A young mother is suckling her son. As he wriggles from her into sudden, heavy sleep, milk spurts from her breast and on to the pages of Volume 7 of Proust's *A la Recherche du Temps Perdu*. She dabs the book with a muslin napkin, buttons herself, reads on, while her son sleeps. She is an obedient woman, a mother, a cleaner, an androgynous reader.

I was also a smoker in those far-off days, who hadn't quite got the face to admit that I might easily have flicked ash into my baby's adorable ear. Even then I was grappling with the impossibilities of motherhood; and I still am. That cornucopia of love and sustenance and approval, selfless and adoring, was also a transgressor, set to be the disappointment all mothers must surely and inevitably be, given the promise they embody and the dangers they are bound to deliver.

The version of motherhood that Aeschylus expressed and which most societies have adopted – that 'the mother of him who is called her child is not the creator, but merely the nurse of the young life which is sown in her' – downgrades the importance of women in the whole process, while reminding us of our duties as carers, teachers, feeders. Battles over contraception and abortion can seem to issue from beliefs that conception and pregnancy are hardly women's business and should certainly not be left to them. Their job comes later. And they'd better be careful. Those words of Aeschylus were uttered, after all, in justification of a son's murdering his mother. And if we survived the breastfeeding there was no reason to suppose we'd be any good at the next bits: playing, homework or the teenage years, let alone our children's adulthood and marriage (or not) and the moment when they may become parents themselves.

There is no end to public discussion of what constitutes a good mother and what makes for a bad one. All those mothers – neglectful or oppressive or pushy or putting down, ambitious or needy or depressed – in their sons' and daughters' novels and autobiographies, for instance, get pretty low marks. Jane Austen's mothers are dead or tearful or silly or snobbish. And the critic Lionel Trilling didn't hesitate to remind us that women generally, in real life as

well as in novels, only 'exist in a moon-like way, shining
by the reflected moral life of men . . . They seldom exist
as men exist – as genuine moral destinies.' Motherhood
doesn't, it seems, confer a soul or a destiny, or, necessarily,
a viable living.

We may get offerings of chocolates and daffodils on

Mothering Sunday, but we're not forgiven or let off most of the blame for chronic dissatisfactions and emotional failures. Mothers (and absent fathers) were thought responsible for last summer's London rioters, as they are for school truants. Recently there have been furious exchanges between women who can't have children and those who can and do. Mothers are accused of being smug, complaining a lot and not being much good at it. And meanwhile, a little paradoxically, there are scientific developments afoot that guarantee children for the infertile and – a really alarming prospect – an end to the menopause and so the possibility that we could go on having children into old age.

Women of all kinds, but especially mothers, are by a long way the losers from the current cuts in social services and public sector work and from alterations to the tax system in Britain. They are being driven out of employment by the need to clock up twenty-four (rather than sixteen) hours a week's work to become eligible for tax credit at a time when those extra hours are unlikely to be available and when paying for child care makes working at all barely, if at all, economically worthwhile. And it is the poorest women who have lost their jobs, the cleaners and the dinner ladies. There has been an overall increase of 19.1 per cent in female unemployment since 2009, the highest rise for a quarter of a century. There are apparently some local authorities where 100 per cent of those who have been sacked are women. A 'Working Mums' survey found that almost a quarter of all working women had left employment last year and that 16 per cent had reduced their hours in order to look after their children, because child care costs have become exorbitant.

The memory I began with is fifty-five years old. Women have come a long way since then, so that it is all the more shocking to see how the current economic and social inequalities are restoring mothers to their old double bind: the source of everything we need and the embodiment of trouble.

June 2012

Being Old in Britain

Easily my favourite old-age statistic has it that if most of us can look forward to living for about ten years longer than our parents, we can also expect to spend the equivalent of eight of those years in hospitals or doctors' waiting rooms, maintaining ourselves. That's seriously approximate as a fact, of course, but useful as a speculative metaphor for what it is to be old these days. And if you add to that all those exercises people recommend we perform at least ten times a day, and the walking and the swimming and the procuring and cooking of only the greenest and healthiest food, we're pretty much back to where our parents were. Is all the time and worry spent on our teeth and eyes and ears worth it? We are even advised to do crosswords in what must surely be futile efforts to ward off Alzheimer's. We could easily spend every minute of those additional ten years simply managing to stay alive.

What does woman want? Freud asked, rhetorically and

a little petulantly. And 'woman', you notice, not 'women'. So, what do the old want? Well, we certainly don't all want the same things, though efforts to mollify us or garner our votes tend to suggest that we do. I suppose most of us want some company and some independence. We get free bus passes and television licences in this country, and some help with our fuel bills. The recent 'granny tax', introduced at the last Budget, freezes the tax allowance for the old, which used to rise each year in line with inflation. The freezing doesn't affect those too poor to pay tax and it means virtually nothing to anyone in possession of an above-average income. The group in between will be unfairly deprived of exactly what gave them some security against rising costs.

A recent report commissioned by the government, but dropped from any immediate legislative plans, describes the provision of care for the neediest pensioners and those ones in the middle as 'broken' and maintains that hundreds of thousands of old people are living in 'misery and fear' because of the cuts in funding and of uncertainty about the future.

At a recent conference in north London, convened by several organisations promoting the interests of the old, the message was clear: the old would like their health and welfare problems dealt with under one roof and preferably by the same people. They are exhausted by – and at times find it impossible – going from doctor to hospital to offices which deal with housing, with care, with pensions, with tax issues. Simply merging health and welfare would cut down on the waiting. It might also mean that some doctors and nurses and administrators would be trained and experienced in considering us as a whole, not just as feet or bladders or necks or, indeed, minds. The old are not only old, they are people with whole lives as well as complex physical and mental needs. They live alone or among other people in ways which are immensely important to them. Accompanying an ill friend to an appointment with a consultant surgeon the other day, we were both moved to tears when the doctor asked him what work he had done before he retired, and then a further question in order to hear a bit more about that work. Those questions are rare.

There are disastrous plans afoot to 'reform' the National Health Service, just at the point when there has been a marked and acknowledged improvement in most aspects of health care and, especially, in the reduction of delays to treatment. But 'choice' is the buzzword, not integration. The Health Service is to be opened to private bidders of all kinds, and the chances of standards being maintained, let alone improved, are very slim indeed, in the view of patients and medical professionals. It is not even clear that these 'reforms' will save money, but they will put money in the pockets of some private providers. Care for the old, whether in their own homes or in residential homes, is funded inadequately and separately from health, and this government, like previous ones over the last twenty years, has done no more than wring its hands at the prospect of a swelling population of centenarians, and has no plans to do anything about it.

So what does this old woman want? First, I'd like a

centre for the old, run mostly by old people, which offers us advice of all kinds. Then, I'd like a young unemployed person, versed in technology (as any such person is likely to be), to visit me regularly and teach me to deal with my computer and my newly digitalised television set.

July 2012

Social Mobility

'Social mobility' has become a new theme and rallying cry in the UK, and a useful distraction. Nick Clegg, the coalition government's Liberal Democrat Deputy Prime Minister, says it's this government's 'central social preoccupation'. They have even imported someone from Blair's government to make helpful suggestions on the subject. None of them is in favour of radical change or legislation. They just want the professions – law, medicine, banking, and so on – to open their doors more invitingly to people from 'disadvantaged backgrounds'. Schools and teachers are blamed, as they always are, for failing to spot and encourage talent, and universities are adjured to accept as students those who have been recipients of 'free school meals' (a euphemism for 'poor'), provided their grades are up to scratch.

None of these new champions associates social mobility with equality, or even with equality of opportunity. Social mobility has always been sluggish in this country, and cuts will have made it more so in the last few years. What has changed beyond recognition, however, is equality, or any general belief that it is even something to work towards. There is now a gigantic difference between the life chances of the richest and the poorest and even between those of the richest and those in the middle.

'Meritocracy', the word and the idea invented by Michael Young in his 1958 book, *The Rise of the Meritocracy 1870–2033*, is back in fashion. Young died in 2002, so he wasn't quite turning in his grave when he wrote in 2001 about the egregious misreadings to which his book had been subjected; particularly, he felt, by Tony Blair and New Labour, for whom 'meritocracy' was taken to be an unproblematically desirable social ambition – a use of the term which effectively turned it on its head.

Young's book is a surprising and sometimes difficult mixture of history, satire and prophecy. It features a crusty narrator, a sociologist writing in the wake of a rioting Britain in 2033, who offers stern Swiftian warnings against the rule of meritocrats. Young wrote in 2001 that he was 'sadly disappointed' by Blair's enthusiasm for the idea. As his book's narrator puts it, 'It is good sense to appoint individual people to jobs on their merit. It is the opposite when those who are judged to have merit of a particular kind harden into a new social class without room in it for others'. These meritocrats 'of a particular kind', Young thought, were likely to be smug in their belief that they are right, and convinced that their own social mobility, and its impetus and trajectory, is the best, if not the only form for everyone else, especially their own children. Our school-leaving examination system is an obvious model. Those who have done well through it will inevitably encourage those of the next generation who have succeeded in the same way. Such an elite, Young predicts, could become more impenetrable for outsiders than a social order arrived at straightforwardly through nepotism. Relying on the largesse of the newly privileged may be riskier even than primogeniture as a mechanism for altering the status quo.

The strength of Young's argument lies in his vision of what would happen to a society, to politics, the professions and the civil service, and above all to education, if merit, as measured principally by grades and exam results, were allowed to be the grounds and the guiding principle of social mobility. It would not only cream off the academically most successful members of the working class, leaving what might then be thought of as a rump sub-class with no leaders of their own, it would reduce education to something like a system for sorting sheep from goats, a marketplace for assessment and certification, with no obligation towards, or interest in, educating the whole population and especially those who were not expected to move up in the world. Such a system relies on mass failure and on the deleterious effects for most people of early competition. As Young's narrator brutally announces, 'Widespread recognition of merit as the arbiter may condemn to helpless despair the many who have no merit.' In Young's 2033 dystopia, socialism has been killed off and trade unions emasculated, while education has become occupied solely with reproducing an elite.

The world Young predicted is frighteningly familiar. We have a 'National Curriculum' which all but private, independent schools must follow and which in its narrowness can seem calculated to turn off all but the most doggedly ambitious students. Local authorities are relieved of their charge of schools, and of their accountability to the communities they serve.

To invoke social mobility in the midst of high graduate and general youth unemployment empties it of meaning if there are no moves to reduce economic and class inequalities. The scramble now at every level is between people who are equally qualified for the job. Those who can afford to stay out of the job market for a time, either in education, or in work for which they are not paid, as interns, will win out just as they are expected to.

August 2012

The London Olympics 2012

This wasn't published because I got it in too late for it to have much relevance. Later I wondered whether Joel simply couldn't bear reading me on the subject of sport and especially swimming, at which I suspect he excels.

When I was fourteen I told a blue-stocking great-aunt of mine that I planned to become an Olympic diver – news that was received with a heavy sigh. I was sure I knew what was needed. I could do a backward somersault and something called a Piccadilly, invented in my school, which required you to jump from a five-metre board to a three-metre one to a one-metre one before diving into the pool (though we talked about yards, then, not metres).

It was 1948, the year the Olympics were last held in London, and it was the 'austerity' version, just three years after the end of the war. I'd discovered where the divers practised (I knew nothing of training or rigorous selection) and I made my way to Uxbridge open-air pool, just outside London, to watch them, with the secret hope that I'd be spotted diving from the ten-metre board and instantly asked to join them. No one took the slightest notice of me, of course; but I remember it as my only brush with the Games going on in Wembley, a few miles from where I lived, in a stadium built in the 1920s. Those were the first Olympics to be televised (the BBC paid £1,000 for the right to do so), but no one I knew had a television set, so my memories – and I do have a few – of jumpers and sprinters and, yes, divers, must be of newsreels watched in cinemas, probably Pathé Gazette.

There were no grand building schemes for those Games, and the athletes were housed in a thousand spare bedrooms. I don't think anyone thought the Games an extravagance. Nor can I remember any tampering with traffic lanes or lights to accommodate the limousines of the 'Olympic family'. So few people had cars in those days. The sun shone throughout, and Fanny Blankers-Koen, the sprinter from Holland, affectionately known as 'The Flying Housewife', was the heroine of it all. What I don't remember is these years and years of preparation, vast building projects, sums of money that have swelled to more than £9 billion, in inverse proportion to the recession and to cuts, and accompanied by unconvincing talk of the 'legacy' the Games will leave us all, of our all being in it together.

I've dreaded these Olympics and so have lots of other people here. There has been a long-running comedy series, very funny, that ridicules the nonsensical language used by the group entrusted with 'delivering' the Olympics 'legacy'. We've grown tired of the clichés and were pretty sure that the opening ceremony would be an embarrassment. As soon as the tickets went on sale it was clear that it would be almost impossible to get any for the events you'd want to see. They'd all be going to sponsors and members of the IOC (the International Olympic Committee), who would stay in five-star hotels at our expense: a necessity, as Dr Rogge of the IOC put it, because they were saddled with the tiring job of handing out medals. One friend bravely budgeted for £800 worth of tickets, and got none; several girls I know, who train seriously as swimmers and gymnasts, have been unable to get in to see the Games.

Complaints like these were not misjudged, nor were they heeded. But I, and plenty of others, have had to eat our words. It began with the opening ceremony, which managed to be funny, generous, interesting and an account of this country and its history which acknowledged some good things (the National Health Service and children's literature, for instance) as well as some bad ones. That the Queen should seem to watch herself fluttering down into the stadium, hat and handbag intact, and in on the act, was a wonderful moment. Hard to imagine Mugabe or Putin standing for such a thing. On the Saturday and the Sunday after that, the men's and then the women's long-distance cycle races went past the end of my road, so that we could watch the earliest and latest stages of their races with our neighbours in the rain.

By now I was helplessly won over. And not just because

GB, as we're expected to refer to ourselves, was winning more medals than at any Games since 1908. I'm beginning to understand the tears, the assurances of 'specialness', the 'amazing, incredible, surreal' experiences these golden young people attest to. I'm trying to understand the byzantine rules of cycling, to imitate the strange undulations of the swimmers as they start out, to distinguish between 'ability' and 'skill' when judging gymnastics. Occasionally, I remember all those young people who worked so hard and didn't reach the speeds and heights required of them, and the ones who got there and didn't win medals. It is, as we're constantly told, a dream, a fantasy, a seventh heaven, but one peopled by oddly decent and down-to-earth men and women. The athletes come out of it all as more honourable and attractive than practically everyone else we're expected to admire these days.

September 2012

Schools under Siege

In 1969, after eleven years in publishing, I started teaching English in a large London comprehensive school. That was a high point for teachers who were interested in educating working-class children; but even then there were friends who thought it masochistic of me to teach, and especially in that sort of school. Teachers – probably because a majority of them are women – are despised in this country, almost as much as social workers; and politicians of every stripe feel it their duty to tell teachers how to teach as well as what to teach. A young, inexperienced teacher will find it hard if she does as she's told and tries to get each one of the thirty five-year-olds in her class reading by teaching them 'phonics'. She's not allowed to use her initiative in such matters, which makes it difficult, sometimes impossible, to develop the expert repertoire she needs if she's to work with children's different strengths and weaknesses.

Just when the number of NEETs (young people who are

Not in Education, Employment or Training) has increased by 8 per cent in a year, Michael Gove, the Secretary of State for Education, is planning to introduce harder examinations for sixteen-year-olds and separate ones for the supposedly less able. No one has ever proved that harder exams make students better at anything, as far as I know. Harder exams simply mean that more people fail them, and so eventually fewer people take them. Gove has already put a stop to essential repair work on school buildings. He has cut funding meant to improve the almost non-existent sports facilities in most state schools (an extraordinary nonsense in a year when, we're told, the London Olympics are about to leave us a rich sporting legacy as well as an economic one), and he has abolished the small living and travel allowance the last government introduced to encourage young people to stay on at school or college after sixteen. At a time when prospects for the young have rarely been worse, discouraging them from staying on at school or college and gathering qualifications – which these moves will certainly do – is criminally foolish.

Gove is given to invoking – grandly and quite unspecifically – high-level research to back his hunches, and he is especially fond of telling us that harder exams, fewer A grades and a return to a more 'academic' curriculum, is what 'top universities' want. 'Top universities', it should be said, have never shown the slightest interest in the education of the majority, and are only concerned about school examinations in so far as they make their job of recruiting the students they want to teach easier. It is true that there are universities which profit financially from their school examinations departments. That has never meant, however, that university teachers have considered the deleterious effect the exam system has on most young people's school experience. Nor have 'top universities' shown much interest in schoolteachers, though virtually all universities in this country, as in the United States, began and grew, and found themselves having to accept women students, precisely in order to train and qualify schoolteachers.

Schooling in Britain has always suffered from this concentration on 'the best'. Not only has this run alongside, and even relied on, massive school failure and an inherited aversion to schooling in at least half the population, it has meant that vocational and technical training is regarded as unimportant and is funded at a lower level than so-called academic courses. Paradoxically, it was Business Studies that were shunned and kept out of 'top universities' in my youth: victims of intellectual snobbery, I dare say. Now they receive funding denied to the Humanities.

Good teachers know that their students only progress when they know what success looks and feels like; and those teachers glory in their pupils learning, changing and ultimately taking control of their own education. Students taking a GCSE examination (the General Certificate of Secondary Education) were asked in a recent Religious Studies paper 'to explain why some people are prejudiced against Jews'. Michael Gove exploded publicly, with the words, 'To suggest that anti-Semitism can ever be explained rather than condemned, is insensitive and frankly bizarre.' Of course it must be condemned, but there is something pretty insensitive and bizarre, it seems to me, about a Secretary of State for Education telling teachers that all they have to do is tell children what they may think and what it would be wrong for them to think. No history, no explanation, no discussion, no engagement with the world those children inhabit or with a future to which they might contribute and in which they might flourish. Let us hope at least that we come riotless through August this year, and let us meanwhile content ourselves with our customary freak storms, flash floods and the curse and pestilence of bankers and politicians.

September 2012

Zadie Smith's London

We began this London summer with a hosepipe ban to make up for three years of drought. At last the ban's been lifted, after the wettest summer on record. But Zadie Smith's new novel, *NW*, which I've been reading as it rains, depends on a London so hot that her characters are bound to open their windows and doors and go out into the street. There are four main characters, all in their late thirties, united by the school they went to and the housing estate where they lived with their families in a part of north-west London where Zadie Smith grew up and where she still lives. Two of the four – the women, Natalie and Leah – are still friends, though their lives have diverged: Natalie towards work in a high-flying City law firm, a rich husband and children; Leah to dull but useful work and a passionate marriage threatened by her determination to avoid having children. Both have secrets that are divulged to us but not to each other, and animosities. The boys they knew at school have had harder lives, chaotic ones, spelled out in poverty and drugs and aimless, ever-changing relations with women and with children. Yet Nathan, one of those boys, had been 'the very definition of desire for girls who had previously only felt that way about certain fragrant erasers'. Three of the four are black or blackish, one is white.

The novel tracks time and change 'with the bright quickness of montage', as Leah puts it to herself when considering her own rapid accomplishment of the things she has to do each day, in a part of the novel told entirely in the present tense. Short chapters provide glimpses and moments rather as memory does. Occasionally, awkward lapses and omissions mimic the abbreviated language of thought and even of dreams, while chance and childhood circumstance work alongside effort and intention to influence these lives. The novel's effect, through its glittering fragments, is to suggest that we can never completely avoid responsibility for one another, that compassion may be corrosive and unhelpful and is anyway not enough, and that we have to accept that people just are who they are, and are explained neither by their race nor their class.

More than anyone else writing fiction about London at the moment, Zadie Smith knows about race and class. In a moving recent interview, she said, 'My feeling is, having lived in different classes, that people want equality of opportunity . . . that's the thing that makes me despair: the idea that people aren't given equality of opportunity.'

London fiction could be said to have become something

of a genre in itself this year; 2012 is, after all, the bicentenary of Dickens's birth, and I suppose no one has ever
written better about London. John Lanchester's *Capital*
measures out in stately fashion the diversity and confu-
sion – and some of the grossest inequalities of London – by
telling stories about the residents of a single south London
street, including a banker, an African footballer and a
lonely pensioner. The banker dreams of his bonus and what
it will pay for, and we're not meant to be sorry for him
when instead of a bonus he is peremptorily sacked. Janet
Davey's *By Battersea Bridge* investigates the backstreets of
west London as places that may contain and protect people
who have escaped other lives to live there.

Zadie Smith's London is teeming, contemporary and full
of talk. Her last novel, *On Beauty*, was thought by some (and
eventually even by Smith herself) to have strained a bit for
the tones and habits of New England academics, though one
of them was from the West Indies. Here she's back with an
arpeggio of London speech that is comic, soaring, true to
life. More than that, though, she creates a believable world
of mixtures and contrasts. London as it really is.

My grandchildren – four of whom would describe themselves as 'mixed race' – appear barely to know anyone at
their schools who isn't. Leah has skin so pale she has to keep
out of the sun. Her beautiful husband is a hairdresser from
French West Africa. Natalie's husband is grand Italian as
well as black. Each of them seems, almost like a Dickens
character, entirely new, someone you've never met before,
who might all the same exist. There's a wonderfully sour

old Leftie postman, gently cross that the young are so uninterested in revolution. This urban world is more than multicultural. The new fusion sweeps across class, and this is what Smith does so well. But the paradox is that her novel should strike such a chord at a time when inequalities of opportunity, of education and of wealth increase by the day.

October 2012

Anna Karenina

This piece particularly irritated one or two of the younger editors at In These Times. *They could not accept the idea that I had any business writing about a film I'd refused to see, and I get their point. It was rather perverse of me. But accepting other people's readings of one's favourite books is never easy, and films have a way of eclipsing the novel they're based on. I wanted to explain why I could never go to see a film of* Anna Karenina.

Perhaps I should say something about this new British film version of Tolstoy's novel *Anna Karenina*, which I don't plan to see. You'll already have read about its being filmed for the most part in an old film studio just outside London, done up to look like a derelict theatre, while the country-side bits were shot on Salisbury Plain. I can imagine, just, that the vast flatness of the countryside Tolstoy grew up in might be managed there. Apparently Keira Knightley, as Anna, achieves what one reviewer described as 'screen goddess' status. Anna's husband, whose sticking-out ears upset his wife so much, is played by handsome Jude Law, and Vronsky by a blond young actor with lots of hair, so he won't need to wear a hat or wear his hair long and brushed over his bald patch as Vronsky does when he is with Anna in Rome and momentarily pretending to be an artist.

Appearances are not everything, of course, and they are by no means the only reason I don't want to see this film, though they are an important part of what one takes from a novel. Tolstoy never tells us much about what his characters look like, but what he does stays in the mind. So a thin young Anna is hard to imagine if you remember that Tolstoy writes about her black hair, 'her rather full figure . . . her full shoulders and bosom that seemed carved out of old ivory, and her rounded arms with very small hands'.

There are bound to be problems about turning very long novels into films. This novel is 900 pages long, and the film lasts for 130 minutes. There have been at least twelve film versions of *Anna Karenina*. Most of the actresses who played her (Greta Garbo and Vivien Leigh, for instance) were thin and blonde, and no one seemed to mind. I haven't seen any of them. I've read the novel four, or possibly five, times in English, and once, most recently, in Russian. This meant having a dictionary as well as a good translation by my side, and it took me over a year. The translation I used is by Louise and Aylmer Maude: old-fashioned but reassuring, not least because the couple knew Tolstoy quite well, and Tolstoy read English, so he may have approved of it. The hardest parts of the novel to read in Russian are where Levin is thinking about modernising farming methods on his estate. My farming vocabulary is not extensive in English, let alone Russian. By far the easiest parts were when women were talking, especially to each other. Tolstoy uses a kind of children's Russian for them, which suggests that they'd not had much of an education, despite being aristocrats or perhaps because of that, though they spoke French fluently. It is difficult to know what Tolstoy was saying about Anna's foray into writing books for children. Tolstoy wrote some himself, after all. I hope he wasn't infantilising her, but was remembering that as well as missing her own son, Anna had creative ability that had not had a chance to flower.

It was clear to me when I was teaching literature to young people that seeing a film could encourage some of them to read the novel it was based on. I have seen versions of Dickens's *Bleak House* and of Jane Austen's *Persuasion*, which, if they were not as good as the novels they were based on, were interesting and worth watching, without blotting out my memories of the books themselves. If I made films I imagine I too might want to make a film of *Anna Karenina*. I don't think of it as sacrosanct, and far from doting on Tolstoy, he often makes me very cross. His women are wonderfully understood at times, especially the ones who are sad and plain. But Anna and Natasha in *War and Peace* come to sticky ends, differently punished, you might say, for their earlier vitality, their natural intelligence and their sexual waywardness. Natasha's punishment is to have too many children and to be congratulated for believing her husband is always right.

Some of the reviewers of this new film version have been taken aback by the director's decision to stage the high-society parts of the novel in an old theatre. Several of them have remembered that Tolstoy famously disapproved of the theatre and once said to Chekhov, 'Shakespeare's plays are bad enough, but yours are even worse.' In fact, I am always struck by Tolstoy's organisation of his novels into scenes that move through time rather as a play does, with no modernist monkeying with the pluperfect, and no flashbacks and very few prefigurings. As readers we all make our own spun-off versions of the novels we know well, and sometimes it is hard to endure the imposition of anyone else's.

November 2012

Seductions

Eric Hobsbawm, the historian I interviewed for *In These Times* earlier this year,* died this week at ninety-five. An affectionate friend and an impressive historian, he had one striking blind spot. He saw no point in feminism and disliked the word 'gender' as feminists use it. About twenty-five years ago, at the tail end of my generation's feminism, or at least after its heyday, I wrote a book called *Seductions*. It was not, I'm sorry to say, an erotic money-spinner, but a feminist polemic, published in the US as well as the UK (a rarer fate these days for British books) in a series edited by Edward Said called *Convergences: Inventories of the Present*. It was a generous act on his part, since I'd devoted a chapter to the absence in his *Orientalism* of women of either the colonised or the colonising sort, with femininity present only as a

* See page 282.

metaphor for the vulnerability of the East to the West. Hobsbawm didn't figure in my book, but he was there in spirit as the kind of British socialist (E. P. Thompson and Raymond Williams were others) who wrote as though feminism, and, indeed, anti-racism and multiculturalism, were distractions from the core problem for any capitalist society: class.

Feminism seems to me to have committed a kind of suicide at about that time, as such movements tend to, torn apart by its varieties of essentialism, separatism, liberalism and radicalism, and exhausted by its efforts to find a place for itself within socialism or, indeed, multiculturalism. I tried to explain in my book how and why women have been seduced into men's ordering of the world and their narratives, rather as Gramsci, the Italian Communist, described how workers were likely to be drawn into the hegemony exerted by their employers, seduced, you might say, by Capitalism, so long as it worked for them. There was even the possibility that women who competed successfully with men were sometimes the first to drop their feminism and the first to uphold precisely those 'standards' which might deny access to other women.

If something I recognise as feminism is hard to find these days, there is no shortage of books (and they are mostly American) signalling *The End of Men* (Hanna Rosin) and *The War of the Sexes* (Paul Seabright). Apocalyptic, anthropological – or evolutionary, in the style of Jared Diamond – these are not feminist books in the sense of advancing a politics on behalf of women, any more than Naomi Wolf's *Vagina:*

A New Biography is. Yet for most of the world, the battle is far from won.

Women and girls are by no means equal to men and boys. Their education, their prospects, their economic position and their political power lag behind those of their male counterparts. It is true that in the West there may be a majority of women who have achieved at least some of the things we asked for in the seventies and eighties. In the UK girls do as well as, and often better than, boys at school and take up more university places. Women constitute at least half of professions like law and medicine and journalism. There is a faltering at the top, as there is at the top of business, finance, the civil service and universities, and a relatively poor showing when it comes to politics. Most of these professions have barely altered their working arrangements to accommodate women's different needs, let alone their strengths, and despite the 1970 Equal Pay Act women's pay is still generally between 5 and 20 per cent lower than that of men doing equivalent work. So far, it is women workers – because they are so often single parents and therefore part-time workers – who are the first to be made redundant as a result of cuts.

This generation of young adults grew up on a wave of economic optimism, and it may be that some of them have not quite woken up yet to the difficulties that lie ahead. If they go to university in the UK they will start their grown-up lives with debts of about £50,000. If they don't go to university they will have only a slight chance of any training or apprenticeship and very poor work prospects. Almost all of them will be expected to perform unpaid work of some kind before they get paid work; and their chances of getting places of their own to live in are far worse than their parents' were. They will probably inhabit a world of greater inequality and fewer opportunities, and some of them seem oddly unmoved by such possibilities. Eric Hobsbawm was a great internationalist and a believer in the young. Sensing a revival of interest in politics among the world's young, he was heartened by Occupy and by the Arab Spring, which he saw as a kind of 1848.

December 2012

Scroungers and Taxpayers

Since this was written more than three years ago it would be reasonable to suppose things had changed, even improved. A fond hope . . .

'War on Want' was a clever slogan that may even have characterised a time when reducing, even eliminating, poverty, here and elsewhere in the world, was a serious hope and a proper endeavour. No longer. Now we in the UK are regaled daily with stories demonising the poor. They are 'shirkers' and 'scroungers' rather than the 'strivers' and 'aspirers' the rest of us are. We are asked to imagine members of 'hard-working families', habitually up at the crack of dawn and shocked to see the drawn blinds and curtains of the family next door, who are work-shy, fast asleep, and ensconced luxuriously in homes paid for by us heroic taxpayers. No alarm clocks for them. And – as they have nothing much else to do and anyway spend most of the day in bed – they are producing children at the rate of almost one a year. This isn't 'fair', we're told. We plan our families and live in homes we can afford, even if we have borrowed rather more than we should have done to do so. New benefit rules and tax credit arrangements have been set in train to deal with this injustice inflicted on us by the poor. 'Feckless' families will be evicted from their homes, and sent to wherever there is cheaper, available housing, regardless of work, schools, family and friends. There is even a move to cut benefit to families who have more than two children.

The truth is that most of the poor are in work, and are getting poorer all the time. If unemployment has seemed to grow less rapidly than expected, this is principally because far more people are working part-time, often at several jobs. It has become essential for almost all women to work, yet more and more women are driven out of their modest part-time jobs by the soaring costs of child care. It has been reliably projected that even if the economy were to grow at a healthy rate from now until 2020, the living standard of the bottom 50 per cent of us would decline steadily during those years. Meanwhile, the pay and benefits of top business executives rose by 27 per cent last year to an average of £4 million each. The coalition government talks about unemployment as if it were a chosen way of life rather than the tragedy it is for so many families these days.

Labour introduced the minimum wage when they were in office. It currently stands at £6.19 an hour. Now there is a move across parties to encourage what is called a 'living wage' of £7.45 an hour (£8.55 in London). Calling this a 'living wage' reminds us that it is not possible, or even meant to be possible, to live on the minimum wage. However, this 'living wage' would not be compulsory for employers, though if it were it would make an important difference to great numbers of their employees. The principal advantage of a 'living wage' in government eyes would be that employers would subsidise the poor rather than the government doing so on behalf of trusty taxpayers, and in the process they'd be turning millions of 'parasites' into usefully covetous consumers. One or two employers have actually gone for it: mostly banks, who have almost no low-paid workers, so it won't bother them. One hotel chain and one or two supermarkets are considering it.

In October, Andrew Mitchell, Government Chief Whip and old school friend of the Prime Minister, David Cameron, was eventually obliged to resign from the government for allegedly swearing at the policemen guarding the gates to Downing Street, calling them 'plebs' and suggesting that they 'learn their place'. His denial that he used the word 'plebs' was countered by the suggestion that no policeman would know the word and could not, therefore, have made it up. There is a new ruthlessness to this class warfare, waged by the well-off and successful against everyone else. Some of it is allowed and justified as a sensible response to 'political correctness', and we are encouraged to sneer at poverty and hardship. People have only themselves to blame. Margaret Thatcher famously opined that anyone still travelling by bus after the age of twenty-four was a loser; and Tony Blair regarded the sons of one of his predecessors as hopeless failures, likely to be a source of shame to their father. One became a school headmaster, the other a high-flying civil servant. Neither were making millions.

In May 2012 Mitt Romney said it was not his job to worry about the 47 per cent of the population likely to vote for Barack Obama, and he explained who they were. They were those 'who are dependent upon government, who believe they are victims, who believe the government has a responsibility to care for them, who believe they are entitled to health care, to food, to housing, to you-name-it'. They sound suspiciously like taxpayers to me.

January 2013

Eighty at Last

I am trying to understand why I wasn't moved to tears by Michael Haneke's beautifully made film *Amour*, which besides winning innumerable prizes has been praised to the skies for its 'unflinching' and realistic portrayal of death and dying and dementia. Rightly so. From its beginning, when the police break into an elegant Paris apartment and discover the rotting corpse of a woman, to the end, when a handsome old man suffocates his beloved wife with a pillow, I watched, mesmerised but unmoved, the slow, relentless deterioration of one and the increasingly frustrated efforts of the other to cope with the situation. The film refuses pity. In concentrating on what this particular couple – refined, anal, chilly – do when they experience these things, it does not set out to make them lovable, and they are neither ridiculed nor pitied.

When *Crazy Age*, my book about being old, was published I was not quite seventy-eight, a bit of an upstart in the old-age stakes. Now that I am, at last, eighty, and have walked my mile and swum my forty lengths, I feel readier to speak for my generation and to admit to recognising a good deal of what goes on in that film. I think often about death and about dying (particularly as I walk and swim), and when I forget words and names I worry that I'm losing my mind and my memory. Most of all, I dread becoming dependent on anyone else and I sometimes hurt the feelings of those who would like to help me. Many of my friends are old too. Some of them have lost children as well as partners, and several of them are losing physical and mental power and contemplating, as a result, frightening changes in their lives: helpers, wheelchairs, stairlifts, giving up their homes. I go to funerals and memorial services, and am apt to feel relief that at least I won't have to organise my own funeral or listen to and mull over conventional words of praise or disparagement.

Hospital nurses and carers are being taken to task at the moment for their lack of 'compassion', particularly for their old patients, whom they are constantly told they must treat with 'dignity'. 'Compassion' and 'dignity' have become problem words for some of us. Everyone who is ill in hospital or cared for in a residential home should – it goes without saying – be treated with kindness and respect. This is as true for babies and teenagers as it is for the old. But no one should be asked to feel grand emotions they don't feel and probably can't feel, and no one should be expected to transform their patients' lives; though they should, of course, be asked to behave well.

Amour reminds us that old age and its particular sufferings are part of human life. Most of us will experience
them, if in different degrees, and if we're to be sorry for
anyone, perhaps it should be for those who don't make
it into old age and would have liked to. The film makes
these sufferings of the old interesting and understandable, but it doesn't pity this old couple and it doesn't try
to make us pity them. Nor does it pretend to confer on
either of them the dignity that they both know they are
in grave danger of losing. I'm not sure that you can confer
dignity on people, though you can be sensitive to their
wish to avoid or disguise the worst indignities of weakness and age.

When my mother was dying, it upset her when doctors and nurses thought only of her recalcitrant body and
ignored the long life she'd lived as a hard-working painter.
She winced at the endearments and the soft-pedalling,
longing to be known and treated as the strong, creative
person she'd always been. I have several friends who campaign for the right to choose when they die and also to die
at home. When, in *Amour*, the husband smothers his wife,
the scene is not unwatchable, but it is ugly. We see her body
twitching, struggling under the blankets. She may have a
vestigial wish to stay alive. That is what the old want those
younger than themselves to understand: that a desire for
life can accompany suffering and defeat, and that what the
old want and feel is no simpler or more clear-cut than it is
for younger people.

Pity and ridicule may be our fault. Too many of us lie

about our age, mimic the young, go to absurd lengths to avoid seeming old. Such efforts are all too likely to make the young feel sorry for us or even find us absurd: the very outcomes we least desire.

February 2013

Food for Thought

On a warmish summer's day, five and a half years ago, my husband announced that he was never going to eat meat again. He'd been reading Peter Singer's book *Animal Liberation*. And that was that. Luckily for me, he seems to have been so horrified by the early chapters that he never reached the ones on the slaughtering of fish, and remains curiously unmoved by the thought of those cunning, feathered hooks or nets full of desperately flailing fishes. Nor did his embargo, I am happy to report, extend to a refusal to eat eggs or honey or cheese or milk, as it does with some people I know, and as it did for a time, I believe, with Singer himself.

I've fed people almost every day of my adult life, but I'm not really much of a cook, and taking meat off the menu has seriously reduced my repertoire. I grew up with wartime rationing: powdered eggs, little bricks of cheese, one joint of beef or lamb for the week, which reappeared as stews and mince from Monday to Saturday. My mother left our ration books with the local grocer, who filled a box with what we were allowed and brought it round in a basket on the front of his bicycle: a lot of tinned pilchards and peaches, as I remember, but plenty of cabbage and potatoes too. An uncle of mine once remarked that rationing, putting little knobs of butter into individual midget dishes with people's names on them, and then monitoring their consumption, had provided interesting work for hitherto idle women, like his stepmother, and that we should, therefore, be grateful to the Germans for that, if for nothing else. I learned to make cauliflower cheese and macaroni cheese in those days, and I started married life with those as my stalwart stand-bys.

I'm reminded of all this every Boxing Day, with its mountain of leftovers requiring the hand of a creative genius or two. In my earliest culinary days I saw a wonderfully funny play by N. F. Simpson called *One Way Pendulum*, in which a neighbour was brought in and paid to eat leftovers; watched patiently doing so on stage for several minutes.

Every year I read with dismay that you're meant not only to make your own cranberry jelly and your own Christmas pudding, but to enjoy doing so and to feel gusts of satisfaction at the pleasure you're giving to others thereby. I buy almost everything ready-made at my local supermarket, which advertises its wares as inspired by famous chefs like Heston Blumenthal, who is known for his snail porridge and bacon-and-egg ice cream; though I do buy a turkey from an old-fashioned butcher, where the salesmen wear boaters and striped aprons.

I wish I could drum up more interest in food, the eating of it as well as the cooking of it. The trouble is that if I'm worrying about the food and whether it's edible I can't listen to people at the same time, let alone talk to them. I'm fortunate, however, to be surrounded by people who are more excited by food than by almost anything else except football. One son filled his diary as a small boy with accounts of meals, ones eaten and ones in prospect, even when they consisted of little more than fish fingers with carrots and mashed potato. My heart would sink when he arrived home from school asking excitedly what was for supper. He sweetly assumed that I'd spent the day planning a menu for his delight, when I hadn't, of course, given it a thought, but had suddenly to produce something, and pretend that it had taken a good deal of time and imagination to do so.

If anything, the men in my family care more about food than the women do and are better cooks and far more extravagant food shoppers. The other son lulls himself from agitation into peace and happiness by concocting delicious curries and risottos. My son-in-law writes novels full of memories of exquisite Indian meals, most of them real ones. And my husband consumes his hummus and anchovies and prawns with as much gusto as he used to his *rillettes* and Spanish smoked ham.

The latest news on the food front is that about as much food is wasted as is eaten in the West: a truly shocking fact in a world containing billions of hungry people. 'Waste not, want not' was a wartime slogan, and indeed it is surprising how little we wasted as children in the war, given the awfulness of most of what we ate. The habit has remained. I never leave things on my plate. Partly this is a result of being neither fastidious nor even very interested in what I eat, provided there is enough of it. Partly it is out of sympathy for the cook.

March 2013

Hilary Mantel and the Duchess

People took sides over Hilary Mantel's lecture and her article in The London Review of Books. *It was clearly more sophisticated to back her account of things and to insist that there was nothing personal in her remarks about the Duchess, who has excelled herself, it's true, with the production of a boy and a girl in record time. I'm afraid I detected venom in Mantel's view of this royal wife and all her predecessors. It's a perfectly understandable venom, but I thought she was being unfair.*

You might think that most sensible people in Britain would want to see the end of monarchy. We could do it gently. The royal family is rich, and we'd let them stay in their castles and palaces; we'd just stop paying for them to do so. It seems quite likely that most of them would be relieved to see the last of their dull duties and their crowns. There's no question that Prince Harry would be relieved, unsure whether he's 'a person or a prince', as he once memorably put it, but certain that it's hard being both. We could, at the same time, do away with ridiculous titles and, perhaps, with the House of Lords, our second and unelected parliamentary chamber, even though, oddly enough, slightly more sense is talked there these days than in the elected House of Commons. So why on earth don't we bin the lot? Inertia, mainly, and possibly the sense that there are more important things to worry about, but also, I daresay, because of what Hilary Mantel calls 'our devouring curiosity' and a national taste for ambivalence.

Mantel is the admired author of two weighty historical novels about the English court in Tudor times, both Booker Prize winners. Now she has put the cat among the pigeons by describing Kate Middleton, aka the Duchess of Cambridge, wife of the heir-but-one to the throne and currently pregnant, as no more than 'a royal vagina', the latest in a long line. Mantel's lecture (published in February's *London Review of Books*), begins with Marie Antoinette and ends with Henry VIII, who, besides having six wives plagued by a variety of gynaecological difficulties, had bodily problems of his own.

The press furore has focused on Mantel's brief description of the future queen of England as 'designed by a committee and built by craftsmen', chosen and accepted by the royal family for her womb (did they insist, I wonder, on a prenuptial medical examination?) and her irreproachable appearance and manners: as thin as a clothes horse needs to be, with 'a perfect plastic smile' and no personality.

This is probably unfair and strikes me as a bit

mean-spirited. Prince William and Kate Middleton met at university ten years before they married. It seems likely that she was reluctant to marry him at first precisely because of the fate lying in wait for royal wives, which must be pretty much as Mantel depicts it, and that affection for her future husband eventually persuaded her to do so. All three political party leaders have leapt to the defence of the Duchess, and several women journalists to Mantel's. One, Caitlin Moran, called Mantel's lecture 'sane and beautiful'; another, Beatrix Campbell, praised it as a feminist critique of monarchy.

Hilary Mantel is a clever writer. Her memoir, *Giving up the Ghost*, which describes the appalling failure of doctors to diagnose endometriosis when she was a young woman, is borne brilliantly aloft by her fury at a fate that has left her with a large, suffering body and an inability to have children. She has always written well about anger, resent- ment, pain, as she does here, when she speculates that Henry VIII's bad behaviour may have been due to his being perpetually in pain: 'historians – and, I'm afraid, doctors – underestimate what chronic pain can do to sour the temper and wear away both the personality and the intellect.'

Mantel's outburst is delivered within a measured and witty meditation on the current royal family, her formal encounters with them, and on the courtiers and monarchs she's been busy writing about during the last few years. She is not the first grandee to attack the monarchy. When Lord Altrincham became plain John Grigg in 1957 and suggested it was time for a change, he attacked the Queen's style of speech as 'a pain in the neck' and deplored her inability to string a sentence together without a text. In 2003, Tony Benn, who had also relinquished his hereditary title, Lord Stansgate, wrote of the monarchy as helping 'to prop up all the privilege and patronage that corrupts our society'.

Hilary Mantel is kinder to her kings and princes than she is to their wives, and she'd be the first to read 'women beware women' as an injunction and a warning. She admits that our interest in these people has something cannibalistic about it, that it is often cruel and even patronising. As Helene Hanff, that passionate anglophile, put it in her book *84 Charing Cross Road*, 'every newspaper in London carried headlines announcing PRINCESS ANNE HAS OVARIAN CYST REMOVED. I mean you're a young girl reared in heavily guarded seclusion and every beer drinker in every pub knows the precise state of your ovaries.' With such little gobbets of information about them all we feel able to imagine their biology and their innermost thoughts, confident that we're much cleverer than they are and that they need constant reminders that without our complaisant adoration they would be nowhere.

April 2013

India

One of my sons has lived in India for more than ten years. He's written books about it; and he's currently engaged on a history of how the rest of the world has imagined or known India more or less from the word go. He nags me to remember my first thoughts about India; if, indeed, I had any. I've told him about Helen Bannerman's *Little Black Sambo*, reading Kipling's *Jungle Book*s and seeing the Korda brothers' 1942 film that was based on them. I must have been nine, and I think it was the first film I ever saw. I thought it was wonderful. I fell in love with Sabu, who played Mowgli, and I envied him, wanted to be him. Far from feeling sorry for that poor little Indian boy, an orphan who was up against it, I thought his life magical.

My other memories of India are scattered. I always knew curry was Indian. It came in a packet with a snake-charmer on it. Curry powder and raisins were used in the war to liven up the remains of the weekend mutton. I don't think

I met any Indians when I was a child, and I remember my puzzlement at hearing a Russian aunt of mine announcing – she was given to significant announcements – that Indians were very good-looking, but she didn't like the pink palms of their hands.

Pink, of course, was the colour of India and of the whole British Empire in our school atlases. I suppose I could have filled in most of the pink bits of the world map when I was nine, because I collected stamps, and even the most exotic ones from Africa and the Far East usually had the King's head on them somewhere among the giraffes and the palm trees. I'm sure I heard and perhaps even used the word 'our' in descriptions of those pink parts of the world. Our school geography lessons, however, ignored all that in favour of a concentration on the countryside round the school, and then only up to a twenty-five-mile radius. We never ventured beyond Portsmouth and Southampton.

Later, when I went more often to the cinema, there were Pathé Gazette newsreels, in which no one explained satisfactorily what the relation was between these small, dark people who wore no shoes and the governors and ambassadors in their cocked hats and gold braid, who seemed to be in charge. Black-and-white images of people working in paddy fields and carrying enormous bundles on their heads were to be found in that yellow magazine, the *National Geographic*. There was always a pile of them in doctors' and dentists' waiting rooms.

I was fourteen in 1947, the year of Partition, and though I remember newsreels about Gandhi and Nehru and, even more clearly, oddly enough, ones about Jinnah, I didn't really understand what was going on: why Muslims were leaving India for Pakistan, and Hindus travelling south to India. Nor, I think, did I know about the appalling massacres that were accompanying the process. But I suppose it was at about that time that I noticed Indians here in London, and at university there were three beautiful Bengali girls in my college. I once heard them teasing each other about which of them was a princess, and which a goddess. I have never been sure whether that was a serious conversation or not. It was in that university town that I first ate in an Indian restaurant, which was called, of course, the Taj Mahal.

By the time my daughter met the man she married, a

Parsi from Bombay, I knew a little more about India. I went there for the first time in 1985 and I've been back several times since. By then I'd learned of my own family's long involvement with India. One ancestor went there to make his fortune in what was then Madras in 1716. He was involved in the building of Fort St George, and became its governor for a time. A great-great-aunt of mine had taught herself Bengali in the middle of the nineteenth century and had written a book about her hero, the reforming Bengali Hindu, Raja Rammohun Roy. My family had maintained links with a Dissenting family in Calcutta. And of course I'd seen those Satayjit Ray films by then, the first of them, the Apu ones, while I was still at university.

My son writes of ancient India as 'a semi-legendary land at the edge of the known world full of riches, marvels and monsters'. He also writes of a modern India, in which cities double in size within a decade, the economy grows almost as fast, yet far more than half of the billion or so people who live there are very poor. Some early visitors, Greeks, reported sighting *Enotikoitoi* (or ear sleepers) whose ears were so big and pendulous that they could curl them around their bodies and use them as sleeping bags. Myth and modernity have always co-existed in India, and they still do.

May 2013

The End of Thatcher

At the moment when it was announced that Margaret Thatcher had died in the Ritz Hotel in London, David Cameron, the Prime Minister, must have been having breakfast and preparing to strong-arm Europe's leaders into concessions for Britain, just as she had done years ago. He must have leapt, mid-croissant, on to a plane for London, where – pink and puffed – he delivered his verdict on our 'greatest peacetime Prime Minister', who, he said, 'didn't just lead our country, she saved it'. This was the message peddled by the BBC for most of the day. Scraps of Beethoven and TV appearances by her 'dry' old guard: ex-con Jonathan Aitken, David Mellor and the sad old Lords Young, Hurd and Tebbit. All told the same story. Britain was 'a country on its knees' in 1979, despised abroad as 'the sick man of Europe', let down by its 'failing state monoliths': the remnants of rampant socialism at home. And then along came Thatcher. And look at us now.

Several hours later the BBC found an ex-miner from Durham, who spoke of 'a legacy of destruction', and a woman who believed Thatcher had 'ruined the country'. Channel 4 News began with dissent and division, and next day the BBC showed brief shots of people dancing in the streets of Glasgow and Bristol and the headline of a local Yorkshire newspaper: 'We can never forgive her'. Charles Powell, one of her advisers, has said that she'd have been disappointed if there had not been demonstrations celebrating her death.

When asked by Gordon Brown whether she wanted a state funeral, Thatcher told him she didn't want to 'lie in state' (who would?), but her funeral next week will be the equal of Churchill's and the Queen Mother's. The streets of London will be cleared, 700 members of the armed forces will accompany the gun carriage bearing her body, and I imagine there will be dancing in the North and in some of the poorer London boroughs. It will cost £3.5 million pounds, most of it paid by the taxpayer.

The fulsome encomia continue, but they've had to make way for a bit of the other. There are women who have spoken and written interestingly and with surprising restraint, about her as, of course, a role model, but as a woman who opposed feminism and may even have set it back in some respects. She once told an interviewer that she wasn't a feminist because she didn't 'like strident females'. Only one woman ever got into a Thatcher cabinet, which was regularly filled with her adoring and often empty-headed male admirers. Shirley Williams, a distinguished elder statesman, has spoken admiringly of the woman's superhuman energy, courage and determination, but also of her gathering hubris over the years, which led to her final ousting by the very men in her cabinet she'd relied on. She seems to have had no women friends, and never mentioned her mother. Glenda Jackson, once a famous actress and now a Labour MP, showed her no mercy in her parliamentary 'tribute'.

Thatcher's death has been a windfall for this government, a marvellous distraction from their cuts and muddles. Yet their contemptuous talk of 'scroungers' and 'shirkers' is bound to remind us of the devastations Thatcher's government delivered in the 1980s to industries, workers and communities across the country, especially in the north. Many of the three million people who became unemployed in those years never worked again, and in all too many cases their children have grown up in the wasteland created by Thatcher's policies, for there have been no concomitant attempts to replace work, repair communities or encourage hope. Council tenants were indeed invited to buy the homes they rented, but those who couldn't afford them were consigned to the worst of such housing, and it was at that point that the post-war house-building boom slowed down, never to recover.

Hugo Young, Thatcher's biographer, wrote about her just before he died in 2003, thirteen years after his book was published:

This woman's indifference to sentiment and good sense in the early 1980s brought unnecessary calamity to the lives of several million people who lost their jobs. It led to riots that nobody needed. More insidiously, it fathered a mood of tolerated harshness. Materialistic individualism was blessed as a virtue, the driver of national success. Everything was justified as long as it made money – and this, too, is still with us.

Russell Brand is a harsh young comedian who was born in the year Margaret Thatcher became leader of her party. He testifies to the effect she had on him as he was growing up in the eighties, as he worries about his 'inability to ascertain where my own selfishness ends and her neo-liberal inculcation begins. All of us that grew up under Thatcher were taught that it is good to be selfish, that other people's pain is in fact a weakness and suffering is deserved and shameful.' Hyperbole and deflation seem inevitable responses to this woman of extremes and contradictions.

June 2013

Really Bright Ideas

As of July 2015, two months into a Tory government, the reductions in benefit and tax credits to families with more than two children are now a reality.

Rather than jotting down their ideas on the backs of envelopes, Britain's coalition government relies on those Eureka moments that come to ministers in the dead of night. Like the imaginative plan to reduce the cost of child care by obliging carers to take responsibility for six toddlers at a time rather than four. Insisting on these carers acquiring additional qualifications in English and Maths will, it is thought, make this perfectly possible. Having usually failed to manage a couple of two-year-olds simultaneously, I can assure the well-named Ms Truss, whose idea it was, that it will take more than that to enable most competent adults to cross busy roads with six small children unless they're in leg irons.

Nurses, we're told, should spend a year learning compassion: best done, apparently, by washing a lot of old bodies. Whether this transformative year is to replace a year of their current training, or be added to it – and who will pay for that? – are unasked and unanswered questions. Our Secretary of State for Education, Michael Gove, fulminated recently in the *Daily Mail* about people like me, who have trained teachers over the years. A bunch of Marxists, he writes, 'enemies of promise' of the kind fingered by Cyril Connolly in his book of that name. In fact, that book is remembered for one line in it: 'there is no more sombre enemy of good art than the pram in the hall'. Children, not teachers, were Connolly's excuse for not writing a masterpiece. Then Gove decided to 'restore rigour' and halt the 'dumbing down' of schools and their 'race to the bottom' with a new harder exam, the Ebacc. This was universally confused with his other idea, the EBacc (yes, with a capital B), and it has now been withdrawn, after rejection by Gove's coalition partners, the Liberal Democrats, by the exam boards, by the teacher unions and, most effectively, by a great number of famous people involved in the arts. Luckily for us, U-turns, abandoned certainties and hopeless muddles are almost as common these days as Eureka moments.

April this year was a cruel month: freezing weather and the arrival on April Fool's Day of the government's 'reforms' (otherwise known as cuts) to the welfare state, which is unravelling before our eyes. Free Legal Aid, a vital feature of the post-war changes, has virtually disappeared.

The National Health Service has been manhandled into dependence on private provision. The Disability Living Allowance is to be scrapped in favour of a 'personal living payment' granted only after regular face-to-face interviews; 1,700 disabled people died last year within weeks of such an interview finding them 'fit for work'. The Spare Room Subsidy (known as the Bedroom Tax) requires families in social housing to pay an extra £14 a week for any bedroom not permanently slept in, or move to a smaller home, of which there are far too few. As a result, 660,000 people (two-thirds of them disabled) are currently threatened with eviction from their homes. Meanwhile, the rich have their own cut: their income tax is down from 50p in the pound to 45p.

On the very next day, George Osborne, Chancellor of the Exchequer, claimed that nine out of ten working families would be better off after these cuts, though the Treasury itself has calculated that only three families out of ten are better off and those three are firmly in the top half of the population. Just as shocking as the string of untruths were the language and the sentiments. 'Reform' and 'fair' have acquired new meanings. The fact that only about 3 per cent of the total cost of welfare goes on the unemployed, while more than 40 per cent of it is spent on the old, makes no difference. For Osborne, the poor don't want to work and so deserve nothing from us 'hard-working' taxpayers. That's 'only fair'.

Look at Mick Philpott, says Osborne. He set fire to his own house and killed six of his seventeen children in the process. Are we, decent taxpayers, really prepared to go on 'subsidising lifestyles' like that? There is talk of limiting child benefit to two children per family. These comments and similar ones from the Prime Minister have provoked outrage, and there is, of course, a good deal of opposition to such 'reforms'. But Osborne and Cameron know all too well what they're doing, and I fear that a majority supports them. Making capital out of Mick Philpott's insane act is not seen as hitting below the belt. We are living in dark times, when other people's welfare and, indeed, the well-being of the whole society, have come to seem a good deal less important than shoring up one's own fortune.

July 2013

Extra Time

Perhaps it's best to see these years after eighty as extra time. Not quite 'Extra Time' as at the end of a football match: time, that is, to get a winning goal or to rely on a 'penalty shoot-out'. But more time than we have a right to expect, time that is unlikely to yield opportunities to score off anyone else, let alone to triumph. I wake up with a confused sense of foreboding, the relics of dreams in which everything is in need of repair and it's my job to do the mending. This year friends have died in what seems like mid-conversation. There are questions I haven't asked, feelings I haven't admitted to.

'Change and decay' are all around indeed, catching and hard to alleviate. My moth-eaten clothes smell of the mothballs that have failed in their purpose. Part of a tooth falls out and the dentist charges me the equivalent of a month's pension to see to it. Montaigne wanted to believe that losing a tooth didn't matter. 'Look,' he wrote, 'here is a tooth which has just fallen out with no effort or anguish: it had come to the natural terminus of its time'. And he wasn't even sixty. A mouse dashes across the kitchen floor and then runs insolent rings round me as I try to entice it with peanut butter into an old cigar box. A leaking pipe in the cellar, and the plumber can't fix it. The pipes are of a size and material, he says, no one has seen in a London house for sixty years. Apparently, I narrowly missed electrocuting myself as I bailed out the cellar and whisked my buckets past the main electrical meter and plugs, which were hanging from a damp brick wall by a single nail. You could put a finger through the rust patches on my galvanised water tank, he tells me, and is about to prove that this is so, but I beg him not to. I spend some of most days mending the plates and cups I've dropped, the chair seats we've sat through, the sleeves that have frayed, and tripping over the hopeless piles of books we are always meaning to give away.

And we're failing to keep up with technology. What on earth would we do with Facebook and all those improbable friends it finds for you; let alone Google Glass, where you could read rude stuff on your spectacles while chatting amiably to those friends? And then so many actual friends are ill. A ten-hour operation followed by chemotherapy seems preferable to 'the alternative' for one. Another is prey to hallucinations. I am reading Oliver Sacks on the subject to find out if there are ways of defying my friend's dreamed-up monsters, with their 'malign and mischievous mockery' as she describes them. We're all worrying about

dementia and whether forgetting names and faces and listening to the BBC World Service through insomniac nights
are signs that we're losing it.

A report from the Institute of Economic Affairs has just
announced that when we retire from work our physical and
mental health improves for a while, but then it deteriorates
rather quickly. There's a suspicion that the report is meant
to persuade people to go on working into their seventies – a
foolish plan, given the appalling youth unemployment figures, though plenty of old people would have liked to retire
later, I know. There must be those who play golf or bridge
and go on cruises until they're a hundred, but the rest of
us may run out of things to do. I haven't quite reached that
point, though I spend too much of each day doing crosswords when I should be mending things, and I listen to a
great deal of radio.

It is from the radio that I learn the extent to which we
extra-timers have become a heavy burden on the state.
The National Health Service, which was working well
a few years ago, is now brought low, and it's mainly our
fault, it seems. Yet the government, which claims to have
'ring-fenced' the NHS from cuts, is still demanding £20
billion 'savings' from the NHS by 2015, so that hospitals
and whole departments are closing. Still, we fill hospital
beds other people need more than we do; and we account
for nearly half the money spent on benefits, though it's the
young and the poor and, of course, the 'scroungers', who
get the blame for that.

More and more of us are crowding into this extra time,

hoping there'll be lots of young people to look after us. But the young are getting fewer and may not want to or be in a position to help us. Someone claimed the other day that the first human being to reach 150 is already alive. I hope it's not me. My mother used to wince a little at the 'marvellous, marvellous' her sheer age could elicit from strangers. There'll be no 'marvellous' for my generation, but perhaps some serious discussion about the legalising of assisted dying.

August 2013

China's One-Child Tyranny

China gets a rather kind press here these days. There's nothing like the prospect of trade and economic success to divert our gaze from its atrocities. In mid-2015, and on the best possible authority, I heard that two hundred human rights lawyers had been arrested there. Yet the Chinese ambassador was to be welcomed handsomely in Cambridge the next week. It is the same with other dubious regimes. When David Cameron, the Prime Minister, visited Kazakhstan in the company of a thirty-three-strong business delegation, hoping to set up £85 billion worth of deals there, he refused to be drawn on human rights. 'Nothing,' he snapped, 'is off the agenda, including human rights.' This government appears to be willing to put human rights pretty low on its agenda, whether it is dealing with Kazakhstan, Saudi Arabia or China.

I've been reading the latest novel by Ma Jian, the Chinese writer whose last novel, *Beijing Coma*, was set within the events of the Tiananmen Square massacre. This one, *The Dark Road*, is about China's one-child policy. Ma's books have been banned in China for twenty-five years, and he has not been allowed to visit the mainland for the last two. He lives in London now with his partner and translator, Flora Drew, and their four children. All this might suggest a writer so incensed by recent Chinese history that he'd be more likely to produce diatribes than novels. But Ma is an artist as well as a writer, which may explain his ability to let us see, as well as smell and follow with horrified belief, the extraordinary world he writes about here and its consequences for one young woman.

Drifting along the Yangtze river, it seems, is a vast flotilla of small ramshackle boats and barges, the homes of thousands and thousands of fugitives from the terrifying threat of family planning officers. The river generates its own foul industries alongside occasional patches and moments of beauty. Corpse-fishing pays well, while 'the pale swathe of floating refuse is still glowing faintly'. Dead babies and aborted foetuses float by or are washed on to the banks to rot. The toxic innards of a million discarded computers – shipped to central China from the West – are crunched underfoot for miles around by a gradually poisoned population, which lives by recycling the body parts of a billion laptops.

At the centre of the novel and of this endlessly and multiply polluted landscape, and of the stench and floating hell of detritus flowing through it, are Meili and Kongzi and their small daughter, Nannan. Meili is pregnant again with what her husband hopes is the son and heir to his Confucian ancestry. They leave their village and their families in order to protect this unborn child. We come to experience Meili's body as another devastated landscape. She is assaulted from all sides: by her indefatigably priapic husband, by the aborters and sterilisers who tear at her, and by the corruption that dogs her efforts and ambition at every turn, so that, inevitably, she too becomes contaminated, though marvellously undefeated.

She is innocent and knowing. Clever, naturally entrepreneurial, a peasant girl with almost no schooling, she longs for the things that gleam at her from the media and that she caught a glimpse of on a brief honeymoon visit to Beijing. She is dazzled, rather as the reader is, by the glint and shine

of the rubbish that surrounds her. Even mountains of plastic bottles and bags can suddenly catch the light and force a sort of gasp from us at their strange beauty. Meili's dreams of what money might buy for her are made up of the same shoddy components and the same visions of happiness and a life where her body – and the children it is not allowed to produce – are at peace. She longs to work, to learn, to grow.

Ma has written elsewhere about the journey he made to confront and research the appalling effects of this policy. His own mother had five children, in response, perhaps, to government injunctions at the time to have as many children as possible. Deng Xiaoping introduced the one-child policy in 1979 at exactly the moment when the birth-rate was beginning to go down of its own accord, partly because of increased prosperity. It is the arbitrariness of the policy that Ma excoriates, the cruelty it encourages, its barbarous interference with people's sexual and family lives and, most poignantly in the novel, its violence against women and girls. It is boys that are wanted, so girls grow up hating themselves, children grow up with no siblings and boys with a much reduced chance of finding a female partner.

A recent official report proudly announced that 336 million abortions and 196 million sterilisations had been performed under the one-child policy. The rich can sometimes flout the rules by paying fines or going abroad; and there are signs that the government may relax the policy, not for humane reasons but in order to supplement the labour force. And a new – one might think and hope, unenforceable – law has been introduced. Every one of those single children must visit their elderly parents regularly.

September 2013

From the Old Country

I keep telling myself that comparing my memories of being young with what seems to be happening to young people now is no way to understand their experience. But how else should I go about it? I know several people as old as I am who eschew such foolishness and are sure that there are no substantial differences between the generations.

Parents and grandparents who are not literate themselves and who watch their children learning to read and write may feel rather as I feel: that the young inhabit a different universe. I can't decide whether we were young in the way people are young today. Was my youth, and even my children's youth, lived somewhere else, in a place that didn't prepare us all that well for this one? Perhaps what's wrong is the habit of starting from one's own memories when you're trying to understand what it's like to be someone more than sixty years younger than you are.

When my grandchildren tell me about their travels, I follow them partly by recalling my own first times away from home; going abroad just after the end of the war, staying with a French family in Paris and then in Normandy, and a year or two later with a German family in Cologne. I remember that the chairs in the French family's *salon* were always covered in ghostly dust-sheets, and that the son of the family had failed his exams and was required to swallow a test tube of blood (source unknown) with his *tartine* and *café au lait* at breakfast every morning to improve his grades, and that he was always given *bifteck* for dinner. The German family I stayed with in 1949 lived in magnificent style, it seemed to me, with goosefeather quilts, cream cakes and a maid. In each case, I was away for a month at least, and it didn't occur to me to phone my parents, though I hope I sent them a postcard to tell them I'd arrived. Perhaps the supposed educational benefits of such visits were thought compensation enough for any worries my parents might have had, and for the terrors I sometimes experienced among these alien beings who were so stubbornly attached to their own language.

I certainly worried a good deal when my children spent their months abroad in the early eighties, two of them in the United States, one in Damascus for several months. Telephoning was expensive, and rarely happened, though by then we'd have thought it reasonable in an emergency. This summer, two granddaughters have, separately, narrowly missed major train crashes in France and in Spain, and have encountered for the first time on their own the bizarre customs of foreigners, especially those to do with food, dress and what counts as pleasure. They were not slow to point out these curiosities, to take photographs of them and to communicate their amazement to literally hundreds of 'friends' from all over the world via Facebook and texting. Throughout their times away they were in contact with parents, friends and even grandparents. And where I am left with one or two indecipherable photographs and boxes full of letters, they will have thousands of photographs of themselves and their friends, but no letters. Will they have what they need to jog their memories and compare their grandchildren's youth with their own?

It sometimes seems that all this instant and easy communication has altered for ever the way we know and relate to other people. Intimacy itself, confiding in others, privacy, solitude, perhaps even conversation, must surely be affected by all this cheap and speeded-up contact. And then everyone's a potential celebrity, responsible for the mark they make in the world, and ready to reveal a carefully edited version of it all to a vast circle of 'friends'. Recent research by Ofcom (the Communications watchdog) suggests that families are more likely to watch television together than they were, and children are less likely to have sets of their own or to repair to their bedrooms to watch them. But this renewed 'togetherness' is not quite what it seems, since every family member, whether young or grown up, brings a smart phone, a laptop, a tablet with them to the communal watching, to create what is apparently called 'media meshing'. There are no more quarrels about channels. Instead, programmes and the discussions they prompt produce 'instant messaging' via social media and texting. We're all getting used to the ceaseless clicking that accompanies meals, journeys, chats; and the heart of the family living-room is now a 'digital hub', delivering as well as receiving an unstoppable flow of news and opinions.

In Britain today, 20 per cent of employable young people have no work. In general, the young have lost more from austerity measures than other groups, in terms of education, financial support and their future prospects. My generation grew up in austerity, but we knew things would get better, and they did. Yet the liveliest memory I carry from my adolescence is, paradoxically, of boredom, of Sundays especially, when everything was closed and there was nothing to do. My grandchildren click their way out of boredom and stay in touch. We live and we learn from them.

October 2013

Seamus Heaney on the Syllabus

Michael Rosen is a polymath who writes witty and devastating polemical articles about education and is often to be heard on the radio talking about language. He is best known, though, for being a 'Children's Laureate' and for writing poetry for young children, which delights and amuses them. Asked the other day why he writes for the very young and mainly performs and reads his poems in primary schools, he replied that poetry is popular with children until they reach secondary school. They like reading it, hearing it, writing it, acting it out. Thereafter, poetry is associated, as Rosen put it, with humiliation. It's the stuff you get tested on, that crops up in examinations. For many people, poetry remains a terrain of difficulty, full of misty, murky deformations of language, requiring esoteric and sometimes desperate decoding skills.

Hearing that word 'humiliation' in relation to poetry on the day after we'd learned that Seamus Heaney had

died reminded me of a time in the early seventies, when he sometimes stayed with us on his visits to London. Occasionally Marie, his wife, came too, and once they both came with their three small children en route to Berkeley, California, where they were to spend the year.

I was teaching English in those days in a large London school, and one of his poems – it was 'Digging', of course – had appeared on an examination paper the year before as an 'unseen' text. We talked about this at breakfast one morning, and I remember Seamus being torn between pleasure that his poem would be read by thousands of young people and anxiety at the thought of the questions those young people would be obliged to answer about structure, theme, form, vocabulary and so on, and whether it was any good. Would his poem remind them of failure rather than success? How off-putting that might be. Perhaps they'd avoid his poems for ever more. So he came with me to school at half-past eight in the morning and talked to the class that had read his poem. As city children, some of them needed more help with the digging than the writing part of the metaphor, and they wondered whether 'snug as a gun' had anything to do with the IRA. I'm pretty sure he said it didn't, and I'm certain that his poem and his visit made a lasting impression that was anything but humiliating.

It was after that, though I no longer remember when it was, that our dear friend Seamus became so famous that you hesitated to drop his name in public. His friends teased him, called him Famous Seamus. When we invited a bookseller in to clear some shelves, the only books he really wanted were the Heaneys. And then there was the late-night knock on our door in October 1995. Seamus had just heard, in the most roundabout way, that he'd won the Nobel Prize. He brought the champagne with him that we needed to celebrate, and celebrate we did. He always had double feelings about his success and his fame. He was a naturally modest man, rather shy and embarrassable, who blushed as he greeted you, but he knew how good his work was and he never pretended not to. He had had a few poems published in Ireland, but none here so far, when my husband, who was literary editor of the *New Statesman* in 1964, published some in the journal. The poems arrived from Seamus with a stamped addressed envelope in case they were rejected. They weren't, of course. But it was a gesture typical of Seamus. Not long after that he was rung up by Faber & Faber, the London publisher.

He came to think of himself, I think, as a lucky man, literally 'gifted', whose duty it would always be to respond to the enthusiasm of his readers and admirers with warmth and generosity, just as it would always be his duty to work as hard at his writing as his father and his grandfather had on the land. His quite extraordinary popularity as a poet (a best-selling poet is a rare creature, after all) was undoubtedly a surprise to him. But he liked reading his poems to people, and talking about poetry, and he probably accepted more invitations to do so all over the world than was good for his health. He liked writing them out by hand as well. Every year there were Christmas cards with a new poem, usually in his own handwriting. The last card we have from him, thanking us for dinner, ends with the words, 'Jaysus! You never know what's next.'

November 2013

Berlin

'Who in all the world goes to Berlin voluntarily?' Joseph Roth, the Austrian Jewish journalist and novelist, wrote in 1920, just as he was preparing to go there himself for the first time. He never got over his hatred of Berlin, but then he didn't much like Vienna or Zurich either. However, it wasn't true then and it certainly isn't true now that foreigners have disliked or avoided Berlin. My Jewish grandparents chose to leave their comfortable Hertfordshire home in 1902 for a longish stay in Berlin, and their first child was born there. And my father, who wasn't Jewish, but who was a musician, spent what I've always imagined were the best years of his life in Berlin in the late 1920s, before he married and before I was born.

Recently, Berlin has become a favourite European city all over again. People talk enthusiastically of its calm, its wonderful museums, its cheap and delicious food and abundant opera tickets. There are still parts of the city where you can buy an apartment with high ceilings for not very much money by our standards. I've just paid it a lightning visit with a much-travelled son, and we were both impressed. Compared with London, there are fewer people, fewer cars and a great deal less waiting around for things. And there are far fewer signs of ostentatious wealth. The public transport system is superb, and you are more likely to be mown down by a man on a bicycle with a child on the seat behind him than by a ten-ton lorry or a Mercedes.

I'm told that unemployment is higher in Berlin than in other German cities: 12 per cent; and that the city is heavily subsidised by those other cities. The government, most of whose departments have now moved to Berlin from Bonn, is a major employer. Heavy industry couldn't flourish in West Berlin during the airlift, and it is only now that industry is getting going again. You get a lot of information because everyone learns English and my schoolgirl German is put to shame.

Yet, between my father's time there in the late twenties and my visit this year, Berlin has undergone such earth-shattering traumas. I caught only a brief and horrifying glimpse of the Holocaust Memorial, a field or car park filled with what seem to be concrete coffins. More moving are the small square brass plaques set into the pavement and engraved with the names of the members of Jewish families who lived in the houses above them. Apparently children study the Holocaust at least twice at school. Knowing how reluctant the authors of the National Curriculum in Britain are even to touch on this country's crimes and follies, I wondered how on earth you would teach German children about atrocities in which their grandparents were almost certainly implicated.

I did my homework before the trip. A 1990 travel guide looked very different from a 2013 one, in which the city's old East/West divisions are scarcely mentioned. There are old hands who deplore this forgetting of the good things that were lost in a merger which privileged everything Western: childcare arrangements, for instance, and greater equality for women. But a new generation seems almost unaware of the old split. The wall is gone. Checkpoint Charlie and some prettified remnants are all that's left of it, and many maps leave the wall out altogether. We found – without even meaning to – that we spent much of our time in what was once East Berlin. Many of the museums are there, and so are some of the city's most charming as well as its ugliest areas.

I read Joseph Roth's *Reports from Berlin 1920–1933* before I went. The pieces are worth reading for the speed and energy they catch from Roth's hectic life as a freelance journalist trying to make a living. They are fierce, satirical, often very funny, and the picture of Berlin as 'a kind of ungovernable building site' still applies. We could see out of our window an angular white apartment block built in the last twenty years, its horseshoe shape framing a bomb-site left over from the war and smothered in wild flowers. Next door was a street of tall, sombre buildings, late nine-teenth century or later, some restored to their old pomp, some awaiting the attentions of a young entrepreneur.

Roth watched the build-up of Nazi power and influence; he warned of its consequences and the seeping of anti-Semitism into every aspect of Berlin life. He left Berlin for ever in January 1933, on the day Hitler was appointed chancellor. Eighty years later, I wonder what he'd make of the popular Joseph Roth Diele café on Potsdamer Strasse, its shelves piled high with copies of *The Radetzky March* and *Flight without End* and the walls covered with photographs of him. The café is next door to one of his many precarious homes, from which he issued the direst warnings and was ignored.

December 2013

Sex and Sisterhood

Exasperation with her Australian family's chilly hypocrisies rocketed Lynne Segal into anarchist student politics at Sydney University in the early 1960s and then into feminism and 'Libertarianism' in 1970s London. She has a long and impressive record as an activist and an academic; and now she has turned to the business of being old. Her new book, *Out of Time: The Pleasures and the Perils of Ageing*, starts from the perils, indeed from the dismay she feels even admitting to her age, and to the disparagement of the old she expects from others and often expresses herself. The word 'ageing', like the word 'elderly', is something of a weasel word, redolent of avoidance. No one, including Segal, is even sure how to spell it, and we do, after all, spend our entire lives 'ag(e)ing'. It is 'being old' that Segal dreads, though she isn't yet seventy and is clearly as vivid and ebullient as ever.

I find the dread surprising, since she has decided to

omit mental and physical deterioration, and even death, as topics in the book, when for most of us those are the aspects of old age that are really frightening. Instead, her principal complaint is that in old age there is a major falling-off of desirability, especially, though not only, for women, while desire may continue unabated. There are not enough people who want to have sex with us, and there may well be none.

'Keep young and beautiful, if you want to be loved,' Segal used to sing 'mockingly' as she marched with her friends in the 1970s. She sings it no more, and she seems to be saying – and I hope she's wrong – that without youth and beauty, women lose such power as they've ever had. In addition, they may lose love, sex, companionship, even friendship. It is, of course, entirely unfair that many single men can find a partner at any age, when women can't as a rule. And that is probably a form of unfairness that might be addressed on the 'personal is political' ticket, though it is unlikely to become an issue for legislation. I can't help feeling that it is much more terrible for a twenty-year-old to think of herself as undesirable than for an eighty-year-old.

We are more the creatures of our generation than we may want to admit. As someone about twelve years older than Segal, I often felt mocked by those young women who were so confident in their demands and their politics. Already into my thirties, with three children and a full-time job, I rarely marched and hardly ever went to feminist meetings. Ignominiously 'sheltering' (as Segal would have it in my own case among others) in a heterosexual marriage, I didn't feel powerful and had far too little time or energy for friendship. Old age has rendered me comfortably *hors de combat* on several fronts, and available for friendships: particularly, as it turns out, with old women who, for a variety of reasons, live on their own. I don't believe that they 'feel suffocated by the apparent pity the coupled up are likely to project on to them', as Segal suggests.

However, despite her fears, and with her customary forcefulness and optimism, Segal recovers her spirits as the book progresses. She does this first by means of generous readings of her elders and her contemporaries, men as well as women, who rage as she does at the diminution of love and sex in their lives, but who also discover pleasures and compensations, as she begins to in her own life. Some of them really do believe, for instance, that they're better writers and artists in their old age than they were when they were young. Some of them, and she lights on Doris Lessing, are maddened by the young, perhaps, as Segal points out, because they remember their delight in their own youthful beauty and how cruel they were to and about the old.

And then Segal finds love and sex again, this time with a woman. It is clearly a success for both of them; their passion sustained by their living apart and seeing each other at six-weekly intervals. There is more than the ghost of a suggestion here that it is men who make old women's lives miserable, by shrinking from their withered and collapsing bodies. I'd have thought that women were at least as likely to notice and abhor our multiple depredations as men are, though they may be readier with emollients and solutions.

January 2014

Adolescence

Tolstoy called his first novel *Childhood* and followed it with
Boyhood or *Adolescence* and then *Youth*. All three read like
autobiography, though they differ from Tolstoy's early
life in some respects. However, there is no doubting their
confessional quality or the intensity of the hero's memories of growing up. Nikolenka, Tolstoy's fictional self, was
fourteen on a calamitous day he remembers for the shame,
the humiliations and the terrors it delivered, and also for
the furious paranoia it aroused in him. Knowing that he'd
brought most of his troubles on himself did nothing to
staunch his despair and his half-hope that since other people
seemed not to love him enough it must somehow be their
fault. The day passed as a devastating storm passes, though
its passions and their damage are not forgotten. Reflecting
on it all later, the grown-up narrator writes, 'I've read
somewhere that children between twelve and fourteen,
who are moving towards adolescence, are especially likely

to commit arson and even murder. Remembering my own adolescence, and particularly my state of mind on that awful day, I easily understand the possibility of the most terrible crime: pointless, with no wish to do harm, done simply out of curiosity and out of a need for action.'

At sixteen, in *Youth*, Nikolenka starts university. He suddenly becomes absurdly snobbish, perpetually worrying about whether his fellow students are, as he puts it, *'comme il faut'*, and whether his own tastes and behaviour are properly those of his class. His studies suffer. In less than three years he has moved from ungovernable rage and self-pity to that other well-known marker of adolescence, the harbouring of simultaneous and contradictory desires: to belong to a group, find acceptance, defeat possibilities of rejection, while, on the other hand, secretly struggling to prove that he is remarkable, different, unique.

A recent article in the *Observer* by David Bainbridge, who calls himself a zoologist of adolescence or a 'reproductive biologist', warns us that whether as parents and teachers or as politicians responsible for education, attempting to tame or eradicate most of the extreme tendencies of young people in their teens, (which may, as he puts it, 'represent a life-stage unique to our species and absolutely essential for its success'), could work to stifle creativity, flexibility and risk-taking. Twenty-year-olds, he tells us, are better than ten-year-olds at everything; and 'during the second decade of life the brain is profoundly restructured into its uniquely complex final form'. 'Most of the evidence,' he writes, 'shows that today's teenagers are altogether more

sensible than their irresponsible, selfish parents ever were.'
He doesn't think this is a good thing.

Not for the first time, both the UK and the USA have
come low on the International PISA tables from the OECD,
which compare the reading, maths and science attainments
of half a million fifteen-year-olds in sixty-five countries.
Politicians here are blaming teachers and schools as well as
each other, and we're shown film of nine-year-old children
in Singapore, who have four or five hours of extra tutoring
after a school day, get to bed at 2 a.m. and rise at 6. It is
they, we are told, who will inherit the future.

It would be gratifying if one could attribute our poor
showing in statistics that are by no means beyond challenge
(even though they are taken so seriously by government
ministers), to a culture in which young people are enjoying
lives untrammelled by curriculum or exams or, indeed, by
the prospect of a life's indebtedness and unemployment.
Sadly, that's not the case, though it's true that teachers are
expected to spend at least as much time assessing students
and predicting their grades as actually teaching them. As
well as doing worse than children growing up in South
Korea, children here are encouraged to compete with
each other at all points and are constantly told where they
stand in the pecking order. It may be that the suicide rates
among the young are higher in these East Asian countries,
but at least their school systems appear to be founded on
the idea that every child should be encouraged to think
of themselves as capable of achieving a lot in their education. Whereas we have a system which pretends to a

level playing-field, while turning a blind eye to the inbuilt disadvantages suffered by a majority of children and doing little to compensate for them. London's mayor, Boris Johnson, has even introduced eugenics into the discussion and a proposal that we should remember IQs and difference when meting out publicly funded education. It's a bit hard to imagine that the children who have the greatest difficulty learning would get preferential funding under such a scheme.

The world's children are all in their different ways being prepared for a global rat race. Our children and yours are apparently 'lagging' behind those growing up in Singapore, Shanghai, Hong Kong and South Korea. No one I've heard yet on the subject has remarked that youth might be a time worth savouring for itself, not just as a rehearsal for adulthood.

February 2014

The First World War

Doris Lessing, the novelist, died last year at the age of ninety-four. She was born in 1919, the year after the First World War ended and the year that a flu epidemic killed several million. The opening chapter of her autobiography, *Under My Skin*, contains the words, 'A war does not end with the Armistice. In 1919, all over a Europe filled with graves, hung miasmas and miseries . . . I used to joke that it was the war that had given birth to me, as a defence when weary with the talk about the war that went on – and on – and on. I used to feel there was something like a dark grey cloud, like poison gas, over my early childhood.'

There are no more eyewitnesses to the horrors of the First World War, so we are in for a centenary year (or perhaps four) of remembering it all at second-, third-, fourth-hand and listening to some ugly debates. Almost all schoolchildren in this country learn at some point about the causes of the First World War or of the Second – topics often used, sensibly enough, I hope, to introduce young people to the problems of historical truth and interpretation. However, Michael Gove, our Education Secretary and a redoubtable ideologue, has announced that the year should be spent 'battling left-wing myths that belittle Britain' and are responsible for what he regards as dangerously unpatriotic satires, particularly the 1963 musical *Oh! What a Lovely War* and the television series *Blackadder*. His counterpart or 'Shadow' in the Labour Party, Tristram Hunt, a well-known historian, has responded angrily that 'attempting to position 1918 as a simplistic, nationalistic triumph seems . . . foolhardy, not least because the very same tensions re-emerged to such deadly effect in 1939.'

My parents were children in the First World War, and my father took a boyish interest in the battles and the map of Europe they so decisively altered. For me and my sisters, that map hung bleakly as the backdrop to the war of our own childhood. There were odd relics from that earlier war: sad, silent men we understood to have suffered 'shell shock', to have been driven nearly mad by what they'd seen. There were pretty women in their fifties with no husbands or children, whose fiancés had died; there were the photographs of two teenage brothers, my mother's cousins, who, we knew, were killed almost as soon as they got to the front, and were remembered poignantly as boys fussed over by their parents, who never let them out of the house without a spare pair of socks, in case it rained.

My parents had friends who had been 'Conscientious Objectors' and went to prison for it, while my grandfather enjoyed his war, riding across Egypt and Palestine as an army doctor with the 2nd Judean Battalion of the Royal Fusiliers. And my step-grandmother, who was to become his second wife, rather gloriously accompanied the Italian army at the end of the war as an official photographer. Then I think of the father of a friend of mine, a Scottish farmer, who took two horses with him when he joined up as his contribution to the war effort. He came back, but I don't think his horses did.

My generation was brought up on the poetry of Wilfred Owen, Rupert Brooke, Siegfried Sassoon, and its ambiguities; because there was excitement inspired by that dreadful war as well as outrage and despair. Doris Lessing's father was handed a white feather by women who didn't know he had a wooden leg. He was not the only wounded soldier who spent the rest of his life hopelessly depressed and sour with hatred of those who'd encouraged young men and boys to enlist or actually obliged them to join up for a war they felt had achieved nothing for them. The mud, the trenches, the rats that gathered in them, are unforgettable images, endlessly re-enacted in films and on television and always shocking.

It is estimated that about 37 million people died in the First World War, two-thirds of them on the allied side, the remainder Germans and their supporters. These are numbers beyond imagining. This year will remind us of the music and the novels and poems and paintings produced in the wake of that war. Several recent books have argued for alternative attributions of blame and heroism, and 'lions led by donkeys' is currently being countered by Gove's extraordinary claim that the Battle of the Somme, during which 306,000 young men died, almost a third of them British, and 20,000 of them on the first day, should be read henceforth as 'a precursor of allied victory' rather than a calamity.

March 2014

Clever Girls

Not many educational statistics are greeted with enthusiasm in Britain, and the yearly announcement that girls are doing better than boys in our school-leaving examinations and that more of them apply to universities, is no exception. This year, 62,000 more girls applied than boys. The questions and the worries are constant and various. Are boys too apt to challenge school values and demands, or are girls too compliant? Is the bias due to there being more women teachers than men at every stage of schooling? Are the differences a response to changing patterns of employment? Women in this country still earn less than men at almost every level, and they are still doing the least secure and the worst-paid jobs. On the other hand, fewer of them may be completely unemployed, so that many of those poorly paid women are, in fact, supporting their families, on the minimum wage or zero-hour contracts, or both.

Melissa Benn, the mother of two high-achieving

daughters, has written extensively on the subject; her latest book is called *What Should We Tell Our Daughters?* She wonders whether girls 'suppress their own questions, uncertainties, furies, hunches and passions. In short, all the things that make individuals interesting'. A mother I know consulted a teacher the other day about her daughter's difficulties with an A-level philosophy course. She was not taking part, apparently, in discussion. 'Perhaps,' her mother suggested, 'she needs to develop and express her own ideas first.' 'Absolutely not,' the teacher roundly replied. 'She simply needs to learn the requisite chapters of her textbook and produce them on request.'

By a curious coincidence I have just read two novels narrated by women purporting to be in their sixties, which look back on the childhood and adolescence of very clever girls who turned their backs on school when they were sixteen. Elena Ferrante, a mysterious Italian novelist who grew up in Naples, has written *My Brilliant Friend* as the first in a quartet of novels. Her narrator, also Elena and born in the 1940s, sticks to schooling. Elena's brilliant friend Lila, however, marries at sixteen and gives up on what might have been a way of escaping from the poverty she was born into. Instead, sex, marriage, children, biology take over. We already know from the first pages of the novel that this choice has delivered neither escape nor happiness. We don't yet know what happened to her childhood brilliance.

Stella, the narrator of Tessa Hadley's *Clever Girl*, is ten years younger than Ferrante's two friends. Growing up in Bristol in relatively genteel poverty, at sixteen she finds herself pregnant by a gay friend who lights off to America, and must forget about reading and cleverness. In her late twenties, however, and by now the mother of two sons by different and absent fathers, a 'choice presented itself as if it had been lying in wait all along. Men, or books? With relief, I chose books.' She studies for a degree, does well and then turns her back once again on study and academia to marry and become an occupational therapist.

I was not an especially clever girl at sixteen, but I recognise something of these girls' experience. An interest in sex and boys always contains the possibility for girls of pregnancy and babies. By the late 1940s, when I was in my teens, most working-class girls left school at twelve or increasingly fourteen, and expected to earn their living at least until they married. Middle-class girls were certainly beginning to think about earning their living, even having careers. Only a minority of women went to university. Most of those of us who did were – perhaps without realising it – deliberately keeping options open, vague, flexible. We knew that if we married we might have to follow our husbands to strange places and that if we had children it would be difficult to be taken seriously at work. Several wives gave up their PhDs because their husbands' PhDs seemed to them more important as well as more likely to deliver jobs and money. I knew girls who soared above other girls and boys intellectually. Some of them restarted their careers after child-bearing. Many took up occupations that had little to do with their earlier academic successes.

I'd like to think that these novels refer to a past long

gone, and perhaps they do. I also delight in the fact that girls are doing so well now, though it is difficult to do that without remembering the millions of girls whose intelligence went undeveloped, disparaged, unused, and the millions of girls all over the world for whom that is still true.

April 2014

The Ambiguities of Care

I wrote this before we'd started to make use of professional carers. For the last six months or so of Karl's life pretty young women from Eritrea and Indonesia and the Philippines would arrive at seven o'clock in the morning to help me. They were charming and kind and almost horizontal with overwork. They could only afford a quarter of an hour with us before rushing off to their next job, which might be miles away. The agency that employed them paid neither their travel expenses nor for the time they spent travelling between jobs. We got their service for nothing because Karl was expected to die quite soon.

My husband is ill and I am now officially his 'carer'. I even get letters addressing me as 'Dear Carer'. 'Carer' is a newish word here and for some reason it makes me uncomfortable. It barely appears in the *Oxford English Dictionary*, and where it does it is in reference to a poem of Robert Browning's published in 1850, in which there is 'a carer for none of it': the 'I don't care a hoot or a straw or a button or a damn' kind of carer. As I child I did the usual amount of 'not caring'. An 'I don't care' from me would be met characteristically with 'Don't care was made to care.'

In assuring us that the word 'care' doesn't have its roots in the Latin *cura* (which means almost the same as 'care') or *caritas*, which does too, the *OED* also reminds us that the word 'care' started from trouble, suffering, illness, and so on, and from Anglo-Saxon. That meaning somehow flipped into 'taking care' to avoid such miseries and then into something like concern, taking an interest in, even liking or loving, and, perhaps, looking after someone weighed down by the cares of the world, who might very easily be oneself. The parting shot of everyone currently visiting us in order to help me be a better carer is, invariably, 'Take care'.

Google tells me that a 'carer' is typically an unpaid helper of a friend or relation. But that bypasses the huge turnover nowadays in courses which claim to train people for the 'caring professions'. In this country, professional carers are usually very badly paid and asked to do the things that doctors and nurses don't do, and to do them in record time. And they are frequently blamed for not doing these things as well as we ordinary people would do them.

In my role as a carer, I am invited to explore my recently acquired identity in seminars and gatherings of other carers. The difficulty there is that, like others in the same position, I would need to employ another carer in order to leave the house to attend such gatherings. Instead, I stay at home attempting to mitigate my husband's woes (he has made a list of these in his diary), besieged by professional carers of different stripes, sent by busy doctors with no time for you. These carers are employed by several institutions – the National Health Service and local Social Services among others – which duplicate each other's offerings, and sometimes appear barely aware of each other's existence. Almost all offerers of care are privately funded these days and their services are then sold to the state in the hope of making a profit, so perhaps it isn't surprising that they seem to be competing with one another.

In one day I may be visited by someone suggesting I get a carpenter to put a hand bar above the bath or a board across it and someone else taking blood or urine samples, while a third will give advice about what are safe quantities of morphine and other painkillers for me to administer, a fourth will propose tempting delicacies I might prepare for my husband, and a fifth will inquire about his and my own spiritual state of mind. These are all carers, and they sometimes spend quite long stretches of time telling me about their own and other forms of care I could make use of and in some cases pay for. They are always young, pretty and kind, anxious to help and concerned for me. And after they've gone, through nobody's fault, nothing much has changed. I have made several cups of tea for them, and am almost too exhausted to take a cup up to my husband, who is the patient victim of all this care and appalled to find himself in need of it all.

It feels rather as motherhood felt. Lots of good advice,

but in the end you have to do it yourself. The patient, like a new baby, is there for you to learn on. And the worst bit of that is that you're supposed to have a natural talent for caring – all decent people have – as all women are expected to have a natural motherly streak. You're also expected to make intelligent use of all that advice pouring out from the professionals, which is likely to be contradictory and prey to fashion. And meanwhile, the object of all this attention is ill, in pain, and not all that interested in the state of your learning curve any more than your first baby was.

May 2014

Choose!

By the end of the 'swinging sixties' I was teaching in a large London school, where the children wore – in principle – what they chose to wear, as there was no school uniform. Almost all the girls chose to wear very small blue corduroy skirts, and the boys chose to wear 'bovver boots' and 'Crombie' overcoats if they wanted to look tough or torn denim jackets and jeans if they didn't. 'Choices' were tribally dictated and constrained by cost. As a teacher who was also a parent at that school, I doubt whether anyone felt they were exercising much choice in the matter.

Yet choice is one of the principal mantras of contemporary democracies, an apparently universal good that contributes to individual well-being. It's as if we're free to choose whether to be rich or poor, happy or unhappy, tall or short, black or white. And when things are going badly for us it's probably our fault for making bad choices.

In principle we're free to choose the hospital in which we give birth and the one where we die. In practice we'll be sent where there's room for us. We may be allowed as many as six 'choices' when picking a local school for our children, and may even be thought to have done well if we get our 'fifth choice'. The advantage, we're told, of denationalising the railways, the post office, fuel providers, water, and so on, is that competition among all the newly privatised companies will 'drive down' (a favourite phrase in this territory) prices and drive up quality, responding to us canny consumers, who will naturally choose the best and cheapest among them. If, by chance, all canny consumers chose the same company (which is perfectly possible, after all) there would no longer be competition and we would no longer have to choose among them. How delightful that would be. Isn't it lucky for the choice merchants that we don't all want exactly the same thing?

It's not just that choice is an illusion in most important aspects of our lives – and that it is more illusory for some people than others – it fails us even in trivial matters. All supermarkets offer a 'basic' or 'essential' range of food, which actually means cheap and no choice, alongside the miles and miles of things from which we're to make our intelligent choices. Most of us face these in a whirl of indecision ebbing towards despair. Eggs, for instance. They're not just large or medium, organic or free range, brown or white, in boxes of four, six or twelve, and combinations of all these. There are eggs produced by

Blacktail hens or quails or ducks. And some eggs are still damp and a bit muddy with small feathers sticking to their shells if they come from grand farms belonging to members of the royal family. Carrying home whichever eggs I finally choose I'm slightly haunted by the thought of those I've rejected on grounds I'm quite unable to justify.

During the war there was only one kind of cheese and one kind of butter. The grocer would carve your ration out of an enormous cube of each. Of course I'm pleased that we've emerged from those austere times, but at what cost of time, energy and uncertainty. And there's a built-in impossibility about choice. There'd have to be hundreds of spare beds in popular hospitals and lots of extra classrooms and teachers in popular schools. Both would swell to proportions that might easily turn them into bad hospitals and bad schools. Instead of all this variety, most people would surely rather know that their nearest school and their nearest hospital were reliably good ones, and that if they moved to another town, there would be a good school and a good hospital there too.

We are often addressed as taxpayers as if we were in a position to choose how our taxes are spent, but we're not of course. One vote every five years hardly gives us choice as to where our taxes go. We may like to think that we choose where we live and the work that we do. Most people, however, have little if any choice there either. Even in societies where choice is ostensibly on offer it seems likely that the greatest happiness of the greatest number would be more easily achieved if we fought for our right not to choose but to be able to expect a high standard of treatment from the law, from schools and universities, and from the health service.

June 2014

Age and Authority

Authority gets younger as I get older. The Prime Minister is younger than my children, and most of the experts and wise men and women who are turned to for advice and wisdom these days had not been born when I started work and had my first child. I shifted in my forties from teaching in school to teaching in a university. The mid-seventies were years when teachers were often out on strike, sometimes accompanied by their pupils. I imagined that once I was translated to the university there would be no more strikes; I was wrong. I remember my embarrassment at marching alongside a banner bearing the impenetrable slogan: 'Rectify the anomaly' – university-speak for 'Pay us more'.

As we gathered at the entrance to the House of Commons, hoping to be ushered in to present our case to a Member of Parliament, I was stopped by a tall young policeman with arms outspread. 'Sorry, miss,' he said with a grin, 'I'm not letting you through.' Darren Murphy, well-known bad boy, who'd run rings round me only two years before at school, was eighteen now and a cheerful member of Her Majesty's constabulary. How satisfying it must have been for him to deny entry to his old English teacher and to have such unquestionable authority over her. That was the moment when I felt I might have missed the boat.

I am reminded of *Educated Working Women*, a book my great-aunt Clara Collet published in 1902, in which she considered the difficulties women faced in pursuing pro-fessional careers. Even in teaching – a career which was relatively hospitable to them, after all – age was a problem:

> Their youth and inexperience are facts constantly brought before them up to the age of thirty or there-abouts, and then with hardly an interval they find themselves confronted by this theory of sudden decay of faculties in women.

Clara was writing about women who would probably not marry or have children. Combining those things with a profession was thought virtually impossible at the begin-ning of the twentieth century for all but a few women with rich and complaisant husbands. In addition, women like Clara thought it undesirable, since it would mean married women (a group she disparaged as likely to be spoiled and foolish) depriving unmarried women of work they really needed. Her 'hardly an interval', a mere slit of opportunity in a woman's life, would be undetectable as well as unusable for all but the most ambitious women.

If we older citizens like to invoke experience as a qual-
ification for exerting our authority from time to time, the
truth is that much of our experience wears out, passes its
sell-by date, becomes redundant. Recently I accompanied
a granddaughter to the bank where I've banked since I
was fourteen. She was planning to open her first account.
Airily, I told her all I knew about cheque books and current
accounts and statements and overdrafts, only to discover
when we got there that she would never need a cheque
book, would barely if ever have actually to enter a bank
and could conduct all financial transactions on her mobile
phone. Sitting in on her interview with the bank manager
put me in my place. I understood not a word that was
uttered. My granddaughter laughed her way through it all.

Invoking one's age publicly produces neither respect nor
attention and is apt to sound plaintive, as if you're asking
for – and deserve – special treatment. And I'm afraid I
remember thinking of old people with slight contempt
because they couldn't run or see or hear very well. Weren't
you supposed to get better at things as you got older?
'You're not very fast for forty,' my five-year-old son once
told a friend of mine as she was running for a bus. I also
thought of the old as likely to be repositories of knowledge,
though I wasn't always especially keen to gain access to it.

The age limit for serving on a jury has now been raised
to seventy-five and universities no longer get rid of their
teachers at sixty-five. Psychoanalysts are sometimes
allowed to practise in their nineties and, more alarmingly

perhaps, there seems to be no age limit for surgeons. While MPs can go on for ever, judges have to retire at seventy, and civil servants, who used to have to retire at sixty, are now more or less obliged to work for another seven or eight years. Raising the upper age limits for some workers has by no means come as a response to old people wanting to work and earn money, but in order to save on state pensions, which account for almost half the government's welfare bill.

Perhaps the old have always had to pay homage to their juniors, to concede their dependence on whippersnappers they remember as helpless infants. But it isn't easy.

July 2014

What is Literature For?

I wrote this just before Michael Gove was moved as Secretary of State for Education. It's possible that David Cameron realised that his friend was noisily dismantling state education, that teachers were in despair and that Gove had become a liability. My indignation was inspired, I think, by the thought of politicians dictating what texts teachers read with their students, but also because English as a school and a university subject has suffered for too long already from the strenuous efforts of all kinds of people to turn it into an easily assessable academic subject.

John Steinbeck's *Of Mice and Men* has been on the examination syllabus for English schoolchildren for more than fifty years. It's probably time for a change. There's been an interesting row here, however, because its removal has been accompanied by the removal of Arthur Miller's *The Crucible* and Harper Lee's *To Kill a Mockingbird*. All three were eliminated by several public examination boards after Michael

Gove, the Secretary of State for Education, announced that children in England should be reading books by English writers rather than American ones.

Of course, there's nothing to stop any young person from reading those books and others that are also now more or less excluded as examination texts: Maya Angelou's *I Know Why the Caged Bird Sings*, for instance, and J. D. Salinger's *Catcher in the Rye*. This is a row about school examinations and about the texts that are sanctified by inclusion in them. These 'American' books have been popular with most teachers and with many of their students, in part because they tackle issues like racism and inequality and growing up in ways which make for lively classroom discussion while maintaining their distance to some extent from the students' particular experiences.

The current row is mostly a matter of outrage that a cabinet minister should have his way with exam boards and dictate what teenagers should study. Gove wants more Shakespeare, more nineteenth-century English fiction and poetry, more rigour and, he says, more breadth. There has been a rush by writers and others to offer alternative lists of books in the wake of his edict, all of them accompanied by the usual range of justifications: that the books they've chosen are 'great' literature, 'classics' even, that they are or were particular favourites in someone's childhood, that they are excitingly contemporary, or not at all contemporary, that they tackle vital themes, or indeed, that they don't and are the better for it. And then there is pleasure.

Most English teachers think as I did that the best bit of

their job is reading stories and plays and poems with young people and engaging in conversations about them. The problem with that is that when it comes to exam time the process is turned into a strange sort of study – 'academic', according to Gove – which entails students learning to write a rare and unnatural form of literary criticism in the form of an answer to a question, sprinkled with quotations that must be learned by heart. Most English teachers will have taught students who are enthusiastic readers by this time. Those students may enjoy writing and be good at answering the kinds of question examiners pose, which usually and disingenuously contain words like 'discuss'. They may even rise to the surely bizarre request that they 'compare and contrast' the Oedipus of the Sophocles play with Kafka's Gregor in *Metamorphosis*, as some of them were required to recently.

But many teenagers are not keen readers, and their English teachers will want above all to change that. A diet of texts that bore them, and a year or so practising writing essays about them, can turn many young people off literature for a long time, if not for ever. I got round all this when I was fifteen by refusing to read any of my set books and simply getting other people (and I was lucky to have them available) to tell me what I had to write. I passed the exam, though not brilliantly. But it also left *Macbeth* and *Kidnapped* (the poems of John Masefield less so) to be read for pleasure and interest at a later date.

Mr Gove's impressive lip would curl, I'm sure, at mention of pleasure. Proposing pleasure in classrooms is a bit like allowing death-cell convicts their own flat-screen television sets. Yet surely pleasure is what we hope young people will come to expect and experience from reading. Without that expectation of pleasure and interest, they will miss out on the humour and the tragedy and the insights that may come from reading literature. But pleasure isn't easy to assess or grade, which is a pity; someone who enjoys reading is likely to know more about literature than someone who has mastered the art of answering questions in five orderly paragraphs. If they are teenagers it is quite likely (though not inevitable) that they will get pleasure from books their teachers and their parents don't like or even approve of. Their pleasure is still the most promising part of all that.

Gove goes in for belief and for shortcuts. He seems certain that young people will believe that the First World War was glorious and that English writers are better than American ones, if they are told as much. I've been reading the memoir of the Czech novelist, Ivan Klima, which tells the story of what happened to banned writers and their work when publishing and journalism and education were controlled by government committees. Those committees decided what should be included and what banned entirely on the basis of what was said or implied in them about how things were going in Czechoslovakia at the time. I recommend the memoir to Mr Gove.

August 2014

A Sense of the Ending

Karl, my witty, beautiful husband of nearly sixty years, has been ill for a long time. Diagnosed with one kind of cancer in 2006 and another (unconnected) in 2009, our local specialist hospital gave up on him this March and sent him home to what is called 'palliative care in the community', which in this case means me and our children. So no chemotherapy and no more radiotherapy or surgery; just lots of free morphine. He sleeps a good deal, has vivid dreams where he and assorted friends swap poems and songs, which he writes down and edits for us when he wakes up. He describes his latest as 'definitely the worst poem ever written'. Threaded through both his sleeping and waking dreams is a constant yet varying anxiety about a lost book or article he's failed to write or to finish or to deliver on time.

While I walk to swimming in the morning, one son draws him curled up on his bed like a snail with surprisingly thin, pale, elegant legs emerging from its shell. When he wakes up, the other son makes coffee and reads poems with him. He and Karl are currently choosing poems by Samuel Johnson and Thom Gunn from a new anthology of poetry about London. And Karl recites bits of 'Tam o' Shanter' and 'To a Mouse' by Robert Burns, and sometimes he sings. Our daughter arrives with a delicious lunch or supper, talks to him and is a comfort to us both. Karl recently told her that he loved her so much he didn't know what to do.

In principle Karl has been sent home to die, but he doesn't seem interested in doing so at the moment, and is even a little better than he was. He quite often comes downstairs for meals these days and he eats well. We've hired a wheelchair for outings, and he gives each of us marks out of ten for smooth steering and avoiding bumps on the pavement.

All this is coming to seem like normality. I try to remember a time when he had two full-time jobs and got home at eight in the evening, and then later when he retired from work before I did and read and wrote in his study and had lunch with friends in restaurants and went to the London Library to collect six books with their labels like shields on the front. But those times are blotted out for me now by this new life. The floor round his bed is silted up with books and magazines he finds difficult, even painful, to read. We've bought a TV set so that he can watch the World Cup on his bed with a grandson.

And there are visitors: old flames, old poets, old

reviewers, old colleagues, old friends, young friends and relations. Karl is pleased to see them, though he worries that he's no longer likely to amuse them. Many of them keep on coming, so I think he does. On the whole I prefer the men, who have no desire to rival or improve my nursing skills, offer tempting recipes or criticise arrangements. One woman worried that Karl was not getting enough in the way of intellectual stimulation, and thought it fortunate that he had sons and plenty of male friends.

He and I don't talk about dying or death, perhaps because I don't want him to tell me that he'd rather be dead, as he has told some of his friends. I don't always tell him what doctors have told me, and I may not show him this account of our current lives. That is probably dishonest

and cowardly of me, but he's not all that interested in the
progress of his illness and is usually happy to down a clutch
of pills or a spoonful of morphine without asking what
he's consuming or why. Cancer often travels mysteriously
and invisibly, and Karl has always been more exercised by
his crippling arthritic pains, which are now pretty well
morphine-assuaged. I sometimes feel that his deafness has
affected our life together more than all his other troubles.
I deal crossly with demands to 'speak up' and then 'don't
shout' and respond rather woodenly to Karl's endlessly
inventive mishearings of what I actually say to him.

I think we are all treasuring this long, strange end of
a life and our part in it, and we cheer up when there are
small improvements, miniature pleasures, memorably
funny moments. We've all slipped into new roles and
had time to adapt to them. I suspect we're much luckier
than people whom death takes by surprise. But I wonder
whether all this isn't an indulgence for us, but unbearable
for Karl. If it is, he's even more stoical than he seems.

September 2014

Peace and War

Like a flock of migrating birds, the world's foreign corre-
spondents move intrepidly and *en masse* from one trouble
spot to another, leaving us with pictures and stories of
unimaginable misery which are hard to forget. I dream of
those hungry families huddled into the ruins of their homes
in the shattered cities they show us: Aleppo, Donetsk, Gaza
City. What's happened to those families we saw? How can
they even begin to rebuild their lives and their houses? But
the reporters have moved on. They have other fish to fry,
and so, of course, have we.

It's been a long, hot summer in London this year, the
hottest since 2006. Postcards arrived from parts of Europe
which were for once no hotter than we were. Far from
envying my travelling, holidaying friends, I've felt grateful
for the peace of an emptied London, emptied of Londoners,
that is. There have never been more visitors from abroad.
But how are we to think of the differences that exist

between what comes to seem like the luxury of peace and the intolerable lives of thousands and thousands of people in those broken, collapsing cities we glimpse on television?

I thought I was getting closer to some kind of answer when I met Mariia, who arrived in London on the 19th of July, the day after the MH17 Malaysian plane was shot to the ground in Ukraine. Mariia is twenty-one. She grew up in Donetsk, and has come here on a six-month visa to live with her aunt's family and perhaps to stay. Her parents have left a demolished flat in the centre of the city for a small dacha twenty kilometres or so outside it. They have no water or electricity there and are living in the cellar below ground, deafened by the sound of planes and bombs and guns above them. They risk being shot if they venture into the garden to find something, anything to eat. They have no way of knowing whose planes and bombs are over-head or even which side destroyed the block of flats they used to live in: whether the rebels or the Kiev government army. Mariia's father would describe himself as a Russian Ukrainian, while her mother's family is simply Ukrainian. Until recently, such things were barely at issue. They are not fond of their own government, but they think of the rebels claiming the Donetsk region as an independent republic as crazy, dangerous people who are at the very least, like them, pro-Russian. They wonder too about their local oligarchs with their private militias, men who own arms factories and mines in Donetsk, as well as sports stadia, some of which have been destroyed, I believe, by one side or the other.

Donetsk made way for the horrors of Gaza and the grey and ragged ruins of a city that looks as if it could never be reassembled. Now the reporters and their cameramen are grappling with those stranded Yazidi refugees on their mountain top in Northern Iraq and the bombs the US is dropping on the Islamic State army who are massacring them.

And woven into this summer of catastrophes is a constant stream of programmes about the First World War, the 'Great War', the war that was supposed to end them all. Sitting here in my comfortable kitchen, waiting for the next bulletin from some torn and ravaged place I shall never visit and then the ceremonial surveying by elderly dignitaries of graveyards in Belgium and France, interspersed with shots of trenches, mud-caked boots, stretcher-bearers, dead bodies, war memorials – it becomes both unbearable and incomprehensible, and my part in it just a guilty kind of voyeurism. It is difficult to believe that we all inhabit the same world. What use is my open-mouthed astonishment at what goes on in the other one?

I've just learned the meaning of a useful new set of initials. FWP apparently stands for 'First World Problem'; this acronym was introduced to me in response to my wailing complaint that yet another curtain cord had been allowed to disappear irrevocably behind the radiator in my kitchen. Briefly back from a stint working in Nigeria, my mocking son swiftly applied a 'Third World Solution' to my weedy problem, unravelling a metal coat hanger and hooking out the recalcitrant cords. I mention this trivial incident in the hope of making some sense of the shocking contrast between my daily preoccupations and the lives and concerns of thousands of desperate people who are simply trying to stay alive and are prevented from doing so by other people, who seem not to know what they're doing or why.

October 2014

Swimming

*Joel and I have talked about swimming – by email, of course –
more than once. We've both swanked about our times and our
lengths. His are inevitably superior to mine: a mile to my kilo-
metre a day. We've both admitted to doing some fairly low-level
mental arithmetic as we swim. Things like: what is the relation
of the lengths I've already swum to the total I'm planning to
swim? How many crawl and how many backstroke lengths have
I still to do? Joel thinks in miles, 'continually calculating what
fraction of a mile I have swum', as he puts it. With so much in
common, I'd imagined swimming was a shoo-in as a subject
for a column, and I was a bit cast down when Joel rejected this
piece in favour of my writing about the Scottish Referendum. He
didn't think his readers wanted to hear about my daily swimming
habits. However, I impressed myself by writing my Scottish piece
and getting it to Joel in two hours. As a reward, I'm including
this.*

I must once have offered swimming as my favourite school subject when quizzed by the bank for security purposes, since if I carelessly offer up anything else – reading, say, or art – I'm told that I'm not who I say I am. (They have also claimed once or twice that I've got my mother's maiden name wrong.) Certainly swimming, if not my favourite activity, has been the main site of competition and competitiveness all my life. Even now, when I'm often cheerfully *hors de combat*, I worry that my swimming times aren't faster than they are, and wonder why so many children and far too many adults are better at it than I am.

My life as a swimmer began, like everyone else's, I suppose, with not being able to do it. I remember watching my father tread cautiously over pebbles on a steep beach in Dieppe, wearing what seem in memory to be hand-knitted trunks as he breasted the waves. I must have been less than three, and I was impressed, though I also remember that he only managed a rather ungainly and worried breaststroke.

Envy colours my next memories. I was five and confined to a large cane perambulator, being regarded as ill and recovering from TB in Broadstairs on the Kent coast. Everyone but me was paddling, swimming, playing in the sand, catching small crabs, and I can still feel how uncomfortably overdressed I was, and my fury that I wasn't allowed out of the pram and into the sea. Then, and most crucially, I returned home at the end of the year to a younger sister I had conveniently forgotten, three years younger than me, who was already diving and swimming like a minnow in our local pool.

I have never worked harder at anything in order simply to catch up — and I just about did. It can't have been much more than a year after that when I watched my mother save that same sister's life as a wave was about to crush her against a breakwater in Sidmouth on the south coast. My sister became less keen on swimming after that, understandably, which hastened my victory while divesting it of some of its satisfaction.

Later on, my school had its own pool, two in fact, though the smaller one was thick with frogspawn and always dark green. The pools were surrounded by a high panelled fence, with the knots of the wood punched out by some of the boys so that they could watch when the girls were naked (compulsorily) on single-sex swimming days. I thrived on everything but that naked swimming, and there was even one summer when I won all the events in the swimming gala, a success never to be repeated, or not by me.

Since then I have swum in rivers shimmering with dragonflies in France and swum across bays in Ireland and Corfu, shoulder to shoulder with salmon and mussels in one and man-of-war jellyfish in the other. I've swum with frogs in a Bombay pool and with dead cows in the Narmada river. And when I was eighty I doubled my daily lengths from twenty to forty in perverse recognition of the battle with bodily deterioration that could no longer be ignored. I'm a slower swimmer now, but a statelier and more efficient one. I used barely to breathe during a whole length. Now I have breathing beautifully worked out, and I don't get tired. My knee replacements make breaststroke impossible, but crawl and two sorts of backstroke make up for that. I know there are Londoners who swim throughout the winter in outdoor lakes, in the Serpentine and the Hampstead pools. They are braver and hardier than I am, and I try not to think about them or mind.

There's an embarrassing gap in my swimming story, actually a gap of about forty years. I decided at sixteen that a concentration on swimming might stand in the way of my being thought an intellectual. It already had, so I dropped it. Foolishly, I forgot to take any of the additional steps that were needed to remedy my reputation in the family and at school as a 'hoyden' rather than a person of serious or bookish tendencies. Other people read books and swam, after all, and I could have swum for my university, perhaps, even become a 'blue'. Instead, I gave up swimming and became a smoker. I probably had a cigarette dangling from my bottom lip as I taught my oldest son to swim. You were allowed to smoke everywhere in those days. And I was an impatient teacher, especially when he refused on every visit to complete the two lengths our local pool required for swimming alone in the deep end. Day after day he would stop, a metre from the end, smile sweetly up at me, and delight in his failure, as I never could.

November 2014

Scotland

Writing about Scotland and its referendum turned out to be a good thing in the end. I was living in a divided house. Karl, my Scottish husband, was appalled at the idea of an independent Scotland, but one son was in favour of it, more ardently so after a visit to Scotland, where he was struck by the strength of feeling on both sides. It would be hard to imagine such passion and excitement down here before any election. This was the last piece that Karl read and edited before he died. It was he who reminded me of 'Tullochgorum'. He particularly liked the first four lines of the last verse:

> But for the sullen, frumpish fool,
> Who wants to be oppression's tool,
> May envy gnaw his rotten soul,
> And discontent devour him!

Scotland will not become an independent country, at least for a while, and I am relieved. It felt like an imminent amputation, though it was always easy enough to see why so many Scots would want to be shot of us. With a recent history of grievances going back to the Thatcher years, when Scotland was used as a laboratory to test the hated Poll Tax and the selling off of council homes, the 'Yes to Independence' campaign clearly made a lot of sense to many people. And as P. G. Wodehouse delicately put it, 'It is never difficult to distinguish between a Scotsman with a grievance and a ray of sunshine.'

Eighty-four per cent of eligible Scottish voters voted (the largest percentage in any election anywhere in the UK since 1951, when I voted for the first time), and among them, also for the first time, were sixteen- and seventeen-year-olds: surely an important and welcome innovation. Yet until a month ago, most of England and the Westminster parliament complacently left Scotland to its own debate in the belief, I suppose, that Alex Salmond and the movement for independence were unlikely to tempt many to abandon the shelter of the UK, the royal family, our place in Europe, in NATO and at the Security Council.

Suddenly and belatedly, a single opinion poll galvanised the 'No' campaign into activity. The three main political parties joined forces to promise all kinds of future powers to Scotland if it turned its back on independence. David Cameron, the Prime Minister, declared that he would be 'heartbroken' if Scotland seceded. Gordon Brown roared back into a form we hadn't seen since Tony Blair beat him to the leadership of the Labour Party in 1994. It was suddenly possible to feel that Alex Salmond would have had a much harder time of it had Labour been in power in London. Of the 59 MPs Scotland sends to Westminster, 41 are Labour, 11 Liberal Democrats, 6 Scottish Nationalists and one is a Conservative. The 'Yes' campaign, which gained the support of 45 per cent of the electorate, must have seduced a large number of traditional Labour voters, most of them probably urban and working-class. The excitement for many of them lay in the possibility that independence would bring progress, fairness, greater equality. There are aspects of welfare and education in Scotland which are already ahead of England, though most of these were put in place by the earlier Labour administration in Edinburgh, not by Salmond. In fact, there has been little in Salmond's career or indeed his harangues to suggest how independence might effect improvements.

Perhaps we southerners do take Scotland for granted. We also take for granted that many of us are likely to be partly Scottish anyway. My husband was born and grew up there and has spent his life writing about Scotland and its literature. My great-grandmother ran the local newspaper in Dunfermline. My children spent all their holidays in Scotland. It was and is a foreign country in many ways, but for three hundred years that foreignness has seemed an asset, a richness, a virtue and a sort of marvel that these small islands could contain such diversity and for most of the time (Northern Ireland has been a grim exception) manage that diversity with good sense. My husband showed me a poem on polling day he'd read as a schoolboy in Edinburgh. John Skinner's 'Tullochgorum', written in the eighteenth century, when Scotland and England were getting used to each other after the union of 1707, delights in telling the old enemies 'to lay your disputes a' aside' and unite.

There is talk now of things being changed for ever, despite the vote in favour of the status quo. Much of that talk focuses on more devolution of power to Scotland, Wales and Northern Ireland, and to parts of England. There is vague talk too of revisiting the 'Barnett formula', which is used to administer and share out grants to the four parts of the UK. Yet this government, like New Labour and Thatcher's before it, presided over the dismantling of the big city councils and the undermining of local government. What has changed is that suddenly everyone in Scotland, young and old, feels it might just be worth voting. In recent years elections, whether national, European or local, have met with the sort of indifference that lets UKIP (the United Kingdom Independence Party, hostile to Europe and to immigrants) win seats in Brussels and locally; possibly at Westminster too. Those of us who feared Scottish independence feared above all that England would be left as a right-wing rump, still given to delusions of grandeur and bereft of those Scottish Labour MPs and perhaps later of Welsh ones too, and damagingly split between the rich south and the suffering north.

November 2014

After Karl

I confess that I was shocked when Joel suggested that I write something about Karl's death and about how I was dealing with it all. It was too soon. I felt tattered, disbelieving, confused. But I thought about it for a bit and began to see that I wanted, even needed, to say something about Karl's actual dying. All the talk and the writing had been by other people, at various sorts of distance. Karl, who was sure no one would come to his funeral or write a friendly obituary, would have been amazed — though still his old sceptical self, I expect — by the warmth of the letters I got and the obituaries and articles about him in newspapers and magazines. And then there was a funeral he might have dreamt up for himself, replete with eccentricities. When my friend from Scotland visited me and told me her Jamaica story, I saw how to write it. There is an awful comedy in being the one who stays alive and has to deal with it all when your closest and dearest person and friend has delivered the unforgivable blow of dying on you. Karl would have been apologetic that he'd landed me with choosing his coffin

and deciding against a sky-blue container for his ashes that was
tastefully adorned with wild geese.

Asked by a neighbour at a dinner party where her husband
was, a friend of mine replied,

'He's gone to his maker.'

'Ah, Jamaica,' said the neighbour, quick as a flash, before
proceeding to deliver himself of quite a long speech about
the history and current problems of the West Indies.

'No,' my friend insisted, 'my husband has died.'

What can people say? What am I to say? My husband
has died, too. He died at home, surrounded by most of
his family, having fallen downstairs after watching the one
o'clock news with me, eating his lunch, and then making
off upstairs to his bedroom and an afternoon sleep. Instead,
he crashed to the ground. When I tell people what happened to him, to me, to our children and grandchildren,
they look stricken, and that's enough.

The Indian woman who lives opposite me shouted across
the street, 'How's your husband?'

'He's died,' I shouted back, twice, because she didn't
hear the first time.

When someone you know and love dies you are confronted by the unique, particular shape of the hole they
leave, by the utter specificity of their absence. That strange,
contradictory, complicated person will never exist again.
Though my husband spent a lot of time writing about 'dou-
bles' in literature, there will be no replicas of him. Yet just
as you're trying to make sense of that you realise you're also

joining the destiny of the entire human race. One death may be very like another and yet everyone everywhere has to go through this experience of a quite particular and unrepeatable loss, one which prefigures your own death, seems to bring it closer and make it less frightening.

All our lives we play with the idea of our own death. Karl was particularly given to announcing that he'd be in his coffin and no one would care, or that he'd be the youngest person ever to die. Or even that he'd rather be dead than . . . Oh, dozens of mildly disagreeable tasks or meetings. Or even 'Over my dead body'. These were in their way 'jokes'. When it looked as though he really might die he talked about it less. But I've been living for several

years now in an almost permanent state of anticipation, of imagining his death, of fear that I'd find him dead in the morning. Yet I was still shocked, taken by surprise, my back turned, my eye on something else for a moment, when he fell downstairs. It is almost as I imagined it but it is also as if I *have* imagined it and it hasn't really happened.

And now I'm a widow. Karl has been dead for more than a month, and I've thought about nothing else. There's been a funeral and a cremation. I became quite friendly with the undertaker, a man Karl would have regarded as 'lacking in affect', who told me that he gave up teaching for undertaking because he preferred adults to children. Dead adults, I suppose he meant. He read *Private Eye* during the cremation. There've been visits to dispensers of death certificates and to lawyers for whom I am now 'the beneficiary'. And I've answered more than a hundred letters and emails.

There is a whole language of comfort and consolation, and by and large it has comforted and consoled me. People I hardly know have hugged me. It has been harder sometimes to digest other people's more public accounts of Karl as an editor, an academic, a writer and set them alongside the jerky hand-held film of our sixty years together as it exists in my head. One woman wrote that having spent her life with a difficult husband she felt for me having done the same thing. Another asked me whether my husband had maintained a positive attitude to life. That was a tricky one to answer. There's been advice: sell your house, take life one day at a time (I had not thought of taking it in any other way).

The worst bit is that I want to tell Karl everything that's happened since he died, what people have said and written. He'd have been interested in who hasn't written. I want to describe the paramedics I called when he fell; the posse of policemen who carried him off to a public mortuary for a post-mortem; the decent, smelly registrar in the town hall. I want to pass on the praise and the criticism, tell him about the funeral in the middle of London, the charming gay vicar who didn't blink when only one member of the congregation joined him in an 'amen', the outpourings of love and admiration, his weeping children and grandchildren. One of my sons told me that he'd cried so much it had cleared his sinuses. Karl would have been so pleased by that.

December 2014

Learning about America

Joel wanted me to write about American politics and how the British view them. But I felt out of my depth, always have, about their electoral arrangements and their system of government, though their presidential elections have always been exciting. So I wrote about my first time in America in 1956 and my memories of politics then.

In January 1956, after four months typing in a London basement to earn the £68 I needed for the fare, I sailed from Liverpool to New York on the *Britannic*, a ship of the Cunard Line. The journey took at least six days, and I was met at the waterfront by my boyfriend, Karl, who'd been at Harvard during those months on a Commonwealth Fellowship. He'd learned to drive since I'd last seen him and been given an ancient Buick, in which we were to proceed nervously along the Merritt Parkway to the apartment he'd found in Cambridge, Massachusetts. He'd hired

furniture for two from the Salvation Army, and the bed
buckled, I remember, on our first night, while the central
heating gushed up at us through vast gratings in the floor.
But it was a charming apartment in a large timbered house
on Hawthorn Street. Our landlord, who lived on the floor
below, arrived next morning to explain to us very politely
that he didn't want sinners in his house. We must either
leave or get married. So we got married at the end of that
week or the next, in the front room of the local Justice of
the Peace, and I have a rather dubious-looking certificate to
prove it. In America then both bride and groom had to have
urine tests to make sure they were compatible. A friendly
urologist Karl had met let me off by taking a double amount
from Karl and putting it in two test tubes. So we'll never
know whether we were compatible or not.

Eisenhower was president then, and in our no doubt
callow way we were pretty sure that even a general as
famous as he was could not be taken seriously as a president.
We were in love with Adlai Stevenson, who was standing as
a Democrat candidate for the second time. We even made
up songs about him. We liked him for being clever, among
other things. By then, though, we were becoming used to
conservative governments. Between 1951 and 1964 Britain
had a series of them. But we were beneficiaries of the six
years before that, when Attlee and his Labour government
had presided over some extraordinary transformations to
health and welfare and education and had nationalised the
railways, the coal mines, the steel industry, and electricity
and water.

Karl's generous scholarship had not allowed for wives at Harvard, so I needed to get a job, and I found one – as a lowly research assistant – with the formidable Professor Carl Friedrich, who, with his research students, was producing a monograph on East Germany. There was often talk – and occasional visits – of a youngish instructor called Henry Kissinger, who, it was hoped, might devote some time to our DDR project. But he seemed always to be in Washington: gallivanting, it was suggested by the woman who ran the department. I learned quickly from her that I should not mention demonstrations or protest songs. Carl Friedrich was famous for writing constitutions for new states, for Puerto Rico in particular, but also for his disapproval of grass-roots movements of all kinds, which he thought of as undemocratic.

There were other reasons why 1956 was memorable for us. Eisenhower was re-elected and our much admired Stevenson defeated again. We had no television, so we only heard about the Conventions in San Francisco from friends who'd been there. We came home to the Suez crisis and a huge demonstration in Trafalgar Square. A police horse gently kicked me to the ground as I shouted 'Eden must go' (my contribution to the protest), but I was unhurt and so was the baby I'd just learned I was carrying. Later that year, the Soviet Union invaded Hungary, and for most of the few remaining Communists I knew that was the last straw, and they left the Party.

They were curious years, those ten post-war years: full of hope and spirit, but still mired in gloom, austerity, sexism and homophobia (though we were struck by how much more devastating that was in the United States, and surprisingly so in Harvard, than it was here). We had not gone through anything as appalling as the McCarthy purges, and race-inspired conflicts had yet to erupt, as they did in London in the summer of 1958. The Cold War was getting into its stride, however, and a lot of those old members of the Communist Party, here, but especially in America, had become passionate defenders of the status quo.

The fifties are often written about as grim and dull, full of repression and discouraging for women. I don't remember them quite like that. I learned something about America in 1956: most importantly, perhaps, that it was a much more complicated place than I'd been brought up to believe, and more 'old world' than 'new world' in many respects.

January 2015

Labour Again?

There's a general election in May and I don't know how to vote. I joined the Labour Party when I was fourteen and left it in 1968 when James Callaghan, who was Labour Home Secretary at the time, refused to allow what he called an 'influx' of Kenyan Asians with British passports into Britain. I bumped into him somewhere once and told him that I'd left and why. He was, of course, spectacularly uninterested. But I've always voted Labour, even when I've had to hold my nose to do so. Now is such a time; though I should add that I've never lived in a constituency where my vote actually helped anyone to get elected. Such is democracy when it's first past the post.

Politics and politicians are at an especially low ebb here just now. The Liberal Democrats have been tainted by their junior role in the coalition government: cuts to welfare and an enormous rise in university fees. The Conservatives are in power, but perilously split over Europe and scuttling in all directions to outdo the new right-wing party, UKIP (United Kingdom Independence Party), which is unlikely to win lots of seats, but certain to unsettle a large number of marginal ones currently held by Conservatives or Labour. And then Labour is undone by the possibility that it has lost the ground it depended on in Scotland as a consequence of the Referendum, besides seeming bereft of policies or plans apart from a 'lite' version of the current government agenda. So they will continue with austerity and with cuts to social services if they get in. They'll go a little more slowly and gingerly perhaps, prolong the agony, and they may bring in a mandatory 'living' wage (which is slightly more than the 'minimum' wage), but probably not for several years. They dare not announce tax rises, apart from a so-called 'Mansion' tax, designed to bleed oligarchs, but a worry for some non-oligarchs, whose houses have doubled in value over the last eight years through no efforts of their own, as mine has. So not a popular tax, but, I believe, a fair one.

But here's the last straw. Any decent Labour government would have removed the 'charitable status' granted to private schools years ago. I remember Tony Crosland boasting when he was Secretary of State for Education in 1965 that abolishing the charitable status of such schools would take no more than a two-line piece of legislation. But he never did it. Their status saves these schools millions in tax and they educate about 7 per cent of the nation's children, almost all of them from wealthy families. Instead of denying them this tax rebate, Tristram Hunt, Labour's Shadow

Education Secretary, has proposed that these schools may keep their charitable status so long as they step in to give a helping hand to their local state schools. Since it is possible to be both unqualified and untrained and spend your life teaching in such schools, where classes are small and conditions of work comfortable, it seems absurd and deeply condescending to suggest that these teachers have much to impart to teachers in state schools, who are used to leaking roofs and large classes containing quite a lot of children who are multiply disadvantaged.

It's true that private schools usually have arts and sports facilities that state schools lack (many of them were encouraged to sell their playing fields for development during Thatcher's government) and might use. But it is typical of this Labour Party and of earlier ones in and out of government that they won't touch this anomalous tax dodge for schools that lies at the heart of the worst inequalities of British society. They won't because some of them went to such schools and even send their children to them.

That 7 per cent of the child population becomes half of the students at the best universities, half of all doctors, half of the House of Commons, more than half of senior civil servants, officers in the army and judges, and so on. And inequality is growing. The gap between rich and poor is not only unjust, it is bad for the economy. Too many working people earn too little to buy the things they produce. We are returning to a 'small state', with spending on welfare heading down towards levels not known since before the Second World War, and reliance on a private sector that is not expanding fast enough to replace public sector jobs, and is not delivering high enough wages.

I will probably vote Labour again in May. There's not much of an alternative. If there's a Green candidate I might vote for her, but she won't get in either, and my vote wouldn't even count then as a protest vote. I suspect that this election will have the lowest turnout of voters since universal suffrage was introduced and that we'll end up with some dismal coalition containing one or two UKIP racists and a few Scottish Nationalists. The public is so alienated from politics at the moment that they seem not to care that we have a government that is threatening free speech, selling off the National Health Service and campaigning to leave Europe.

February 2015

Widowhood

Joel turned this down. Perhaps he'd had enough of me on the subject of Karl's dying, and anyway he wanted something on UKIP instead.

One day soon I shall have to give a widow's banquet to thank everyone who has taken me out, given me lunch or dinner, worried about my welfare since Karl died. Too stunned at first to do much more than acquiesce, I am waking up now to my obligations. I have felt protected. No one is going to disagree violently with me so long as I am this mournful thing, a new widow. When asked how I am I answer simply 'All right' or even 'Fine', because I am; but I live in a strange place, talking silently a lot of the time to someone who isn't there; though his ashes, well-wrapped and boxed, are upstairs in the sitting room, waiting for their scattering in the Pentland Hills south of Edinburgh in the autumn. Karl felt the cold and would have warned us against venturing anywhere much in cold weather. We'd thought of the Isle of Wight because it was once planned as their next destination by Andrew O'Hagan for his annual visit with Karl and Seamus Heaney to a poet's home: Tennyson's in this case. But we've thought better of it. The Pentland Hills are where Karl bicycled as a boy and where the subject of his first book, *Cockburn's Millennium*, lived with his family in a house called Bonaly.

My sister has given me her cast-off iPad, and I'm busily trying to discover hitherto unknown needs it might satisfy, unsuccessfully so far. And my daughter has given me an enormous photograph album. Though I've never taken photographs I've accumulated thousands of them, which I try to date and then choose the best among them. In fact, I do remember taking one photograph. It was of Karl gaping in amazement at the Grand Canyon. But my photograph omitted his head and the Canyon and just caught a sign saying 'Scenic view ahead'.

One son is collecting the drawings he did of his dying father and making a book of them. The other is trawling letters and scrapbooks for a story of his father's life and friendships that might illuminate his own. I too am reading old letters, gazing at photographs, puzzling at cuttings and snippets in the hope of making sense of my long life with this person I sometimes feel and, of course, always felt, I didn't really know. This was not because Karl was especially unknowable, but because some sort of gathering incomprehension has accompanied the intimacies of married life for me. It's much easier to think you know a friend than to give a coherent, believable account of a life's partner.

Karl's letters to me were written during the few times we were apart when we were young, and they're filled with complaints in the early days and children and gossip later on. 'Abroad' generally got a bad press from him, and my letters to him are full of assurances that Salzburg or Harvard can't really be as bad as he found them at first. And I was right. Once he'd met people he was happy, though perhaps 'happy' is too strong a word. Neither of us ever got used to being alone, and he never was for long.

People tell me that this is mourning, that it lasts a long time, moves in stages, is changeable and unpredictable, and I suppose it is. It veers between hollow disbelief and regret. The regret is that I never quite told him how lucky I always knew I'd been in my life with him. That was not the sort of thing we said to one another.

Some people have told me that all this gets worse. I sense a reluctance to relinquish it, as if that would constitute the final abandonment, confirmation that I have a future and Karl doesn't. It isn't all sad. It's bewildering and strange, not least because I have such difficulty believing in its finality, in the eternal absence of this particular person, or thinking about what that means for me at my age, with still another bit of life to live. But finding evidence and stories about Karl before I knew him or in the bits of his life I was not part of gives me pleasure: childhood and adolescence, his National Service spent reviewing films and books for the British Forces Network radio in Hamburg, football (playing as well as watching), work.

An old friend casually remarked the other day that

widows were famously unreliable witnesses to their dead husbands, whether as 'keepers of the flame' or vindictive termagants. I demurred politely, but I imagine that I might not be the ideal contributor to a biography. We are rarely experts on our spouses' childhood, and if we are critical we are likely to be differently critical from colleagues or rivals.

I have, however, discovered a use for my iPad. To my astonishment and after some random button-pressing it suddenly delivered a radio programme I thought I'd missed about Karl's earliest best friend at university, the poet Thom Gunn. There wasn't much in the programme about those early days, but it prompted me to remember them for myself.

March 2015

UKIP

There were boys in the London school where I was teaching in the early seventies who couldn't wait to leave school and start work. They did not welcome the raising of the school-leaving age to sixteen in 1972, and were occasionally given to teasing us teachers for accepting what they thought of as low wages for an uninteresting job. In those days they were mostly vindicated, as there were real jobs for them, and I don't remember thinking that we were sending them off into unemployment. That changed in the eighties. I had left school-teaching by then, and I often wondered what happened to those lively and perhaps over-confident boys when Margaret Thatcher laid waste to manufacturing in this country and broke the back of the trade unions in the process.

One answer is offered by *Revolt on the Right*, an academic study of the history and current condition of UKIP (United Kingdom Independence Party) by Robert Ford and

Matthew Goodwin. Founded in 1993 as a single-issue pressure group dedicated to taking the UK out of the European
Union, UKIP has mutated erratically over twenty years to
become a populist right-wing party that is seen as a serious
threat to the three main political parties and to the future
possibility of any government having a majority, which may
or may not be a bad thing in itself.

UKIP now appeals, according to the book's authors,
to what they call 'left-behind groups' – more men than
women, most of them over fifty-five, white and working-
class – who have come to see 'a cosmopolitan, multicultural
and globalised Britain as an alien and threatening place'.
Many of them have been unemployed or underemployed
for years. Few had much education beyond the age of sixteen. Paradoxically, the authors suggest that these UKIP
supporters are often a good deal less interested in the issue
of EU membership than in UKIP's hostility to immigration
and to Westminster politics and politicians. A majority of
them once belonged to trade unions and voted for 'Old
Labour': Labour, that is, pre-Tony Blair.

In defining this group, the authors see it as a sympto-
matic aspect of tumultuous social change in this country
and in some other Western countries too. We've simply
come later to this shift among working-class voters from
left to extreme right, than France, for instance. The
authors contrast the country that voted in Harold Wilson's
Labour government of 1964, when almost half the work-
force did blue-collar work and 70 per cent had no formal
educational qualifications, with Tony Blair's 'New Labour'

election in 1997, when less than a third of the population had working-class jobs, trade union membership had dwindled from 40 per cent to 20 per cent, and only 50 per cent had no formal educational qualifications (a figure that is even lower now).

Since this book came out last year, two Tory MPs have defected to UKIP and been returned to parliament in by-elections. By far UKIP's greatest success, however, is in being represented by twenty-four of the UK's seventy-three elected MEPs (Members of the European Parliament) in Brussels and winning 163 seats in the most recent local authority elections, though they have not yet won control of a single council. The expectation is that UKIP will field candidates in almost every constituency in May's general election, though we may be protected from having Nigel Farage (the Head of UKIP) as our representative on earth by our 'first past the post' electoral system. Membership of UKIP and possible voters for it have grown, but most people suspect that it will be difficult for them to win many seats, since their support and those 'left-behind groups' are spread across the country rather than huddling in any one constituency.

Ford and Goodwin have written an admirably dispassionate and well-researched book about this new political party, its history and its possible future. There are lacunae: not enough about the party's financial backers, nor about the related weakening of the unions and of the working-class worlds many of these 'left-behind' people once looked to. I should have liked more personal testimony from people who have moved towards UKIP. However, the book makes up for that by describing the creation of a new political party (and they compare this at moments with the brief successes of the Social Democratic Party in the 1980s) from the viewpoint of those who are doing it, so that we get interesting insights into internal disputes and into UKIP's perspective on the exploitable vulnerabilities of the main parties.

This is in many ways a dismal story of our times, though it's possible to feel that it is less the growth of a right-wing politics that is surprising and dismaying than the thought of lives so blighted by unemployment and by people's sense of being unheard and powerless that they are prepared to vote for a party as chaotic and negative as UKIP.

April 2015

London Jihadis

That mysterious and terrifying figure in his balaclava, wielding a serrated black knife as he prepares to cut off the heads of journalists and missionaries from the West, always had a recognisable London accent, which is why he was nicknamed Jihadi John. Now that he's been identified as Mohammed Emwazi we are no less baffled. Described as 'quiet, reasonably hard-working and aspirational' by his head teacher at a school I once knew as chaotic if well-intentioned, he was remembered by another teacher as in need of anger management. I may have glimpsed him sulking in the back row of a classroom there. Apparently, he was bullied and short of friends in those days. He complained later that MI5 had threatened him and 'put words in his mouth'. He is remembered for getting blind drunk and abusive on his journey from Somalia to Syria and as 'cold' and 'a loner' by fellow Jihadis. Other scraps of information have him as 'the best employee we ever had' according to a Kuwaiti he worked for, a petty criminal in his teens and 'painfully shy'. An IT graduate who once had ambitions to be a footballer, he is likely to have suffered some ineradicable ignominy in his childhood: his family were Bedoons, an ethnic group which is denied full citizenship in Kuwait.

We are no wiser and probably never will be. As we worry about just who indoctrinated Jihadi John and those three London schoolgirls who slipped across the Turkish border into Syria recently, presumably to become Jihadi brides, all hell rages across northern and western Iraq and eastern and northern Syria. These initially parochial-seeming concerns have brought home to us how deeply we're implicated in all this. The government responds with schemes to spy on students in universities, lecture the young about 'British values', and with denials that British foreign policy, racism or revenge for Iraq have anything to do with it. Its so-called 'Prevent Strategy' has, it seems, trained 130,000 people to identify and prevent extremism. Dal Babu, until 2013 a Chief Superintendent of Police, describes its tactics as 'toxic'. Most of the Prevent recruits are white and regarded with suspicion by many Muslims, and as intimidating and unhelpful by those who are confronted by them.

I've been reading the journalist Patrick Cockburn's *The Rise of Islamic State: ISIS and the New Sunni Revolution*, and he doesn't pull his punches. It's been nearly impossible for journalists to report from 'ISIS' territory, which, Cockburn suggests, has 'been convenient for the US and other Western governments because it enabled them to play down the extent to which the "war on terror" had failed so catastrophically in the years since 9/11'. This he attributes above all to the West's refusal to confront their allies, Saudi Arabia and Pakistan, after 9/11. Not only did almost all the 9/11 perpetrators come from those countries, but in seeking to remain on good terms with Saudi Arabia for economic reasons, the West has ignored that country's exporting of arms and extreme Wahhabist Islam.

It happens that I've been listening to yet another voice on the subject. Aimen Dean (not his real name) has been interviewed on BBC radio and television in the last week. He grew up in Saudi Arabia, and as a devout Muslim went to Bosnia when he was sixteen and ended up with Osama bin Laden in Afghanistan, where he recruited al-Qaeda volunteers and taught them to read and write and learn something about Islam, of which, he says, they knew little. His change of heart followed the 1998 bombings of American embassies in Dar es Salaam and Nairobi and the huge loss of life in both places among Africans unconnected to the embassies. Since then, and until fairly recently, he has been a double agent, working for MI5 and continuing to teach young Muslims about Islam, some of whom may choose to fight for al-Qaeda or ISIS. Asked whether he sleeps easily, he assured his interviewer that he did and that he saw it as his duty as a Muslim to save the honour of Islam as it suffers its current 'identity crisis' and to 'extend Islam's existence in the West'.

As you'd expect, Aimen Dean's testimony has been greeted with some scepticism and wonder. It's hard to imagine how he could live safely in the UK after his appearance on television or how he could allow his young students to consider becoming suicide bombers or murderers in Syria or Iraq, which some of them may have done. I believed him and was moved to think of the courage and intelligence such a person must possess to try, as he has, to get something right in this impossible conflict.

May 2015

Detained at Her Majesty's Pleasure

There are at least thirteen detention centres in the UK, where migrants may be sent while waiting to hear the fate of their applications to remain here or waiting to be deported when they've been denied asylum. According to the Home Office, there are at least 30,000 people detained for an indefinite period in such centres at the moment. There is nothing illegal about such detention. However, the UK turns out to have by far the worst record in Europe when it comes to the length of time people are kept in such centres, the absence of a time limit on their stay there, and the fact that some detainees are employed in the centres themselves on much less than the minimum wage. Among those detained are pregnant women, children, old people and disabled people, who get poor medical care and little educational or cultural assistance. Even in France, which has a reputation for treating migrants badly, forty-five days is the most that anyone can be held in a detention centre. In the UK, as one young woman in flight from a forced marriage in Sierra Leone put it, 'Every day you spend there, it is like you are in prison, but you don't know when your sentence is going to end. We count the days. It is a waste of your life.' It is unlike a prison in that almost no visitors are allowed.

While campaigners for the main parties compete to show how tough they are on immigration, accusing one another of laxness at border controls and failure to hit targets for reducing the numbers of immigrants allowed into the country, a cross-party committee of MPs has published a report which concludes that the current system of holding migrants indefinitely in what are now known as 'removal centres' is 'expensive, ineffective and unjust'. Their inquiries also found evidence to confirm detainees' claims of abuse and inhumane conditions in many of the centres, which are mostly run for profit by private companies and are largely unaccountable.

One indignant peer in the House of Lords recently pointed out that many migrants come to this country because they are gay and have been obliged to leave one of the seventy-eight countries in the world where it is illegal to be gay. The report suggests that gay men and women fare especially badly in their attempts to remain here. Either they are not believed or they are discriminated against. There is also evidence that the Home Office is pretty random in its response to applicants, and its officials dig in their heels when migrants appeal, even though they may well have mounted a stronger case the second time round.

Some detainees will, however, make it. They may even get to the point of applying for British citizenship. To do so they will be expected to achieve at least 75 per cent in the compulsory test and to swear allegiance to this country, with God or without. The test consists of multiple-choice questions most of us would find difficult to answer, though they could be mugged up. Migrants are expected to know about the Vikings; when farmers 'first arrived' in Britain (conjuring an image of fully fledged yokels landing at Plymouth, armed with pitchforks and with straw in their hair); land ownership in feudal times; Henry VIII and his six wives; and when exactly our seventeenth-century Civil War began. They are also asked whether British people eat duck, chicken, turkey or ostrich at Christmas. These are British values, it seems, without which we'd be nowhere.

I wonder whether someone detained in a 'removal centre' for months or years, without knowing when they're going to be let out, would respond 'true' or 'false' to the statement: 'You must treat everyone equally, regardless of sex, race, age, religion, disability, class or sexual orientation.' Or how they'd choose between 'it is your right', 'a criminal offence' or 'your responsibility' to 'cause harassment, alarm or distress to someone because of their religion or ethnic origin'. They will answer, of course, as they think we want them to.

The world is full of refugees. The UK has accepted only 143 Syrians so far. Faced with genuinely life-or-death issues, most people would lie or cheat to give the right answers, to be the migrant Britain welcomes. No wonder, really, that a young man I know from Ethiopia was advised by an older friend to construct an entirely false narrative about his life, in the hope of being allowed to find work and stay here. His applications to remain in the UK have been refused several times. After five years of living more or less on the run, with no source of income and dependent on the kindness of friends with sofas or spare beds, he has abandoned his story and is about to return to Ethiopia.

June 2015

Democracy

I was unfair to the Tory government on one thing: they have pro-posed introducing a 'living wage' – though not until 2020 (when there will be another general election) and not for anyone under twenty-five.

I shall be eighty-seven when I next vote in a general election, the principal manifestation, I suppose, of the many 'shrivelled forms of democracy' available to us, as Noam Chomsky put it. I know I should be grateful for living in a country where people are able to express and vote for diametrically opposite things. Yet this 2015 election delivered the familiar thud of disappointment, as I expect the next one will. It's possible that this one was more etiolated than usual, a matter of grossly misleading opinion polls beforehand, and hasty and unconvincing post-mortems afterwards, and no serious proposals from anyone to improve things. For instance, how miraculous it would have been if an elected government offered before anything else to take its fair share of those refugees who have survived the crossing from North Africa to Europe after nearly drowning in the Mediterranean.

The election itself has given us an even more right-wing version of the status quo and, of course, the surprise of Scotland. It's not, I should make clear, that any of this has especially dire consequences for the old, since both the main parties, Tory and Labour, are relatively tender of our feelings, knowing that we're a good deal more likely to vote than the young are. It's the future for the young we need to fear.

A so-called majority government elected by just 24 per cent of the registered electorate will complete its dismantling of the welfare state, the privatising of the National Health Service and its wrecking of the state education system. It will tell us that it is in favour of hard-working families and refer to itself as practising 'Blue Collar conservatism'; but it won't insist on a 'living wage', nor will it invest in the sort of housing programme that would provide jobs and a decent standard of living for those workers they're so busy ogling. It will proceed with its withering austerity policies, cutting £12 billion from what's left of welfare and at the very least take us to the brink – and possibly over it – of leaving the European Union, mainly in order to curtail the arrival of migrants from Europe. There are plans to ditch the Human Rights Act of 1998 (whose principles are adhered to by every other European country except Belarus) in favour of a British Bill of Rights Act, whose sole purpose is to make it easier to ban and deport more of those suspected of harbouring non-British values.

Yet I am obliged to accept that more people wanted those things to come about than wanted the alternatives. Labour and the Liberal Democrats are licking their wounds. The Lib Dems always knew that entering a coalition with the Tories might result in their destruction, and it has. Labour is listening to the mantra of 'aspiration and inclusion' in its search for a leader who isn't Ed Miliband (he is thought by the old guard to have focused excessively on inequality and unfairness). Ed and his family have gone for a well-earned holiday on the island of Ibiza, leaving an unpleasant trail of newspaper headlines of the 'Red Ed' variety and jokes about his tussles with a bacon sandwich, which are probably covertly anti-Semitic. Four million people voted for UKIP (United Kingdom Independence Party), but managed to elect only one MP. And our only Green MP, the admirable Caroline Lucas, increased her vote. Opposite but valid reasons, perhaps, for reforming our voting system from 'first past the post' to some kind of proportional representation.

Only Scotland, in its usual awkward way, has been interesting. The Scottish National Party lost the referendum for independence last summer, but they have made up for it by achieving a near clean sweep in this election. Scotland has only one MP from each of the Tory, Labour and Liberal parties; the remaining fifty-six are Scottish Nationalists. They are now the third largest party in Westminster and could cause all sorts of trouble there. I find myself hoping very much that they will, though the encouragement that will give to their achieving independence may be a heavy price to pay. They won't want to leave the European Union. They'll object to renewing Trident (Britain's nuclear weapons programme) and to having it based in Scotland, and they'll certainly oppose austerity.

The latest tally suggests that 61 per cent of those who could have voted did so, and that a similar percentage appears to want to change the voting system. It's all a bit of a mess. I'm not as a rule given to quoting Churchill, but perhaps I will now. 'Democracy,' he pointed out, 'is the worst form of government, except for all the other forms that have been tried from time to time.'

July 2015

Treacheries at Teatime

Our old friend Eric Hobsbawm, the historian, died in 2012 when he was ninety-five. Two years later, MI5 (the British domestic security service) released the file they'd kept on him since 1942. It consists of about 1,000 pages, goes up to 1963, and there's almost certainly another eleven years' worth of it still to come. His file is thought to be one of the longest of the quarter of a million such files assembled by MI5 over the years, about 20,000 of them on people like Eric, who'd been members of the British Communist Party. Though he admits in his autobiography, *Interesting Times*, that he would have worked for the Russians in the 1930s if they'd asked him to, all that steaming open of letters and listening to phone calls turned up nothing to which he'd not admitted and that his friends didn't know already. He was often maddened and bored by the Party and irritated that his membership deprived him, he believed, of having anything interesting to do during the war. But he stayed in the Party long after 1956, when almost everyone else left. This, he suggested, was because the Party replaced the family he'd lost when his parents died in his adolescence – 'we belonged together' as he put it, not quite a family, but a 'fraternity' – and besides:

> Losing the handicap of Party membership would improve my career prospects, not least in the USA. It would have been easy to slip out quietly. But I could prove myself to myself by succeeding as a known communist – whatever 'success' meant – in spite of that handicap, and in the middle of the Cold War.

Another old friend, James MacGibbon, very much an old-style 'gentleman publisher', served in the Intelligence Corps and reported for work at the War Office in the spring of 1941, a month or two before Hitler invaded Russia. It seemed to him that he had a duty to inform Russia as our ally of what Britain knew about German plans and movements: information that the British government was not prepared to offer Russia, on the grounds that we were likely to be at war with the Soviet Union ourselves before long. James and his wife were also members of the British Communist Party. But, as he told his son Hamish years later, 'I never felt that I was acting for the Communist Party, as indeed I was not. It was to help the war effort.' The MacGibbon household was checked out by a local policeman, accompanied by his wife and two Special Branch officers, when James started work at the War Office. He was cleared by his superior officer following a brief exchange which he related to Hamish forty years later:

'Are you for Stalin or for us?'

'For us, sir.'

'Shake on it.'

The MacGibbon phone was bugged for years. No one,

however, seems to have overheard James or his wife Jean saying anything in the least incriminating, and he continued to live his rather charmed life to the age of eighty-eight.

Cathy Massiter, a British whistleblower who worked at MI5 from 1970 to 1983, revealed that whereas only one person dealt with possible right-wing subversion, there were dozens dealing with civil-rights organisations, nuclear disarmers and trade unions. She saw this as a reluctance to see left-leaning groups and individuals in the thirties and later as above all 'anti-fascist'. She even suggested that there were old hands in the Service who thought of fascists and communists as being pretty much the same thing.

Though my husband's mother joined the Communist Party in her youth and I had relations who did as well, neither my husband, Karl, nor I were ever Communists. Nevertheless, we attracted a strange kind of surveillance in the seventies, when a handsome American would join Karl and his footballing friends to watch Saturday afternoon matches at Stamford Bridge, the Chelsea ground down the road. He always brought a delicious Sachertorte for our tea afterwards. His interest in football seemed slight, and we came to the conclusion that he was hoping to catch some of us uttering treacheries at teatime. Though he wrote for the newspapers from time to time his reason for living in London was never explained, though we learned later that he was employed for many years by the Congress for Cultural Freedom, which was funded by the Fairfield Foundation and the CIA.

The Lives of Others, that mesmerising film about Stasi

surveillance in the old East Germany, commiserated understandably with the secret service agent, stunned with boredom as he listens in to weeks and months of domestic trivia, probably missing the clues he's meant to detect and report on in the process, and is eventually seduced by the much more interesting lives lived by those he's spying on. I always hoped that our cake-bearing guest felt he got his money's worth.

August 2015

The Labour Party in Defeat

Jeremy Corbyn finally mustered the thirty-five parliamentary party backers he needed to become the fourth candidate in the Labour Party leadership contest. You probably haven't heard of him (he's not even very well-known here) though he has been MP for Islington North, a characteristically mixed inner-London constituency, for thirty-two years and increased his already large majority at this year's general election by 6 per cent, receiving over 60 per cent of the vote. When the four candidates for the leadership appeared recently on television, the studio audience (described as people 'open to voting Labour') and even those parts of the right-wing press given to calling him 'an unreconstructed Trotskyite', seemed to favour him, especially when he spoke of Labour having lost its way. 'We have been cowed by powerful commercial interests,' he told them, 'frightened of the press, frightened to stand up for what we absolutely believe in.' Yet it was

241 The Labour Party in Defeat

instantly assumed, not least by Corbyn himself, that he hadn't a ghost's chance of winning the leadership and that his presence on the hustings was simply there to encourage debate. I have just rejoined the Labour Party in order to vote for him.

Corbyn is sixty-six and an old friend of Tony Benn. He is known, among other things, for claiming the lowest expenses of all MPs: £8.95, it is said, for a printer cartridge. He has been consistently and coherently against wars, from Vietnam to Iraq and Afghanistan. He campaigned for the Guildford Four and the Birmingham Six (two groups imprisoned for IRA terrorist acts in the 1970s), who were eventually exonerated and freed. He has opposed austerity with vigour, campaigned for at least partly renationalising the railways and for building affordable housing. Above all, he has argued for the redistribution of income and for greater equality. As a recent *Guardian* profile put it, 'The thing about Corbyn is that he is nearly always proved right – after the event.' He is now almost alone in having these views in the parliamentary Labour Party and being so unequivocally against virtually everything Blair stood for. He probably has about three parliamentary allies.

Corbyn is a decent man and a good politician. He didn't want to lead the party, and it seemed that there was no chance that he'd be doing so. Suddenly, he's ahead: hundreds of people, most of them young, have rejoined the party in order to vote for him. It's surely worth wondering why.

In a recent review of Anthony Atkinson's *Inequality: What*

Can Be Done? for the *New York Review of Books*, the French economist Thomas Piketty highlights Atkinson's argument that the rise in inequality in the UK – which has gone from European levels to ones he describes as 'quasi-American' – can be traced back to 1988, when Margaret Thatcher reduced the top marginal income tax from 83 per cent to 40 per cent, without 'bringing adequate corresponding benefits to society at large'.

Meanwhile, and magisterially, Tony Blair urges the party to embrace 'ambition and aspiration as well as compassion and care', and to go for the centre, ignoring the left and opposing UKIP. He rightly points out that 'leading the debate over why Britain should stay in Europe offers a great chance' to seek out alliances and forge that centre. But he has also advised anyone whose heart goes out to Corbyn 'to get a transplant'. On immigration, he gnomically declares, 'We're for rules, not prejudices.' He is readier to talk of 'reforming' public services than of opposing the £12 billion cuts that the Conservatives are proposing.

Corbyn's style and emphasis put inequality and attempts to reduce it at the heart of Labour commitments. The other three candidates (two of whom – Yvette Cooper and Andy Burnham – are ex-ministers, while the third – Liz Kendall – is a newcomer) are principally concerned with setting out their past and present relation to Tony Blair's New Labour, with its backing for Bush's Iraq War and its partial privatisation of education and health, in the best possible light. They are anxious to sound tough on immigration and to appeal to almost everyone.

Since rejoining the party a fortnight ago I have received invitations to meetings and gatherings and been told, for instance, that Yvette Cooper is a person of experience, who has progressive ideas and espouses Labour values. We have not been informed about the nature of those ideas or values.

Labour, virtually obliterated in Scotland by the Scottish National Party, may well have lost taken-for-granted ground there when the Tories accused them of planning a coalition with the SNP. Some of us thought that Labour was unnecessarily determined to deny any such possibility; since those who know Scotland well seem sure that more old Labour voters were persuaded by the SNP's opposition to austerity than by the possibility that there would be another referendum on Scottish independence.

Those of us the *Guardian* rebukes today as nostalgic for 'a programme of prelapsarian socialist purity' may be deemed naïve and unrealistic. But it's hard not to wish at least for some strong and coherent opposition to government plans to lower the top rate of tax, to alter the method of calculating child poverty in order to disguise its increase and to lop £12 billion from an already shredded welfare budget.

September 2015

Elena Ferrante's
Neapolitan Novel

Part of the mystery and fascination of Elena Ferrante's four-volume Neapolitan novel lies in our never being sure whether this is fiction tricked out as autobiography, or the other way round. It's a vast novel about two women's lives, their work, their relations with men and with their children, and it's also about the effect on all these things of schooling, education and literature, and it takes the two friends at its centre from their birth in 1944 to their late sixties.

I don't think I've read a more intelligent and imaginative novel about contemporary women's lives, nor one that articulates so bravely the difficulties inherent in such an enterprise. The two friends at its centre make this possible: Lila and Elena, two girls born in the slums of Naples, meet on their first day at school. They are opposites and alike, Lila 'very bad' and dark, Elena just 'bad' and fair.

Lila brilliantly clever, Elena clever and diligent. The novel entangles them through the men they love and the children they bizarrely share. It also sends them in different directions, sets them up as rivals, opponents, each other's first critic.

Elena continues her education, becomes a novelist, travels the world, learns to speak standard Italian, marries into the liberal intelligentsia. Lila marries a local grocer while still in her teens, never leaves Naples, and is successfully and locally entrepreneurial in the developing IT industry. For all her brilliance, and though she is recognised as a powerful woman in the neighbourhood where the girls grew up, she is frustrated and imprisoned in her life, while Elena seems free to choose how she lives. Their lives diverge in the earlier volumes, but in the last one, *The Story of the Lost Child*, Elena returns to Naples, stung by unhappiness and at an impasse in her writing. The two women become pregnant at the same time, and Elena moves into the apartment above her friend's.

History and politics are significantly present in these lives, and so is the Camorra, Naples' very own Mafia. The kidnapping of Aldo Moro by the Red Brigades and the 1980 earthquake mimic and affect the tumultuous relations of the two women and the political hatreds simmering in the neighbourhood. In all her writing (she wrote three extraordinary novels before embarking on this mammoth one), Ferrante has been at her most ferocious and candid when writing about being a mother and being a daughter. In a recent interview for the *New York Times*, she said: 'Children always remain an inescapable knot of love, of terrors, of satisfactions and anxieties.' Desperate feelings of love and of disgust, horror at how intimately children remain a part of their mother's bodies even as they pull violently away from them: these are contradictions and crises in which she excels. Rage is her forte, but it isn't a righteous rage. In fact, she goes past women's rage to suggest that beneath a pardonable indignation at what life throws at many women there may lurk a dangerous malevolence waiting to burst out and do maximum damage. It may be a necessary malevolence.

Elena in the novel becomes a successful writer, famous, rich, in demand as a speaker. Ferrante is now famous too and admired all over the world. But she refuses to publicise her books or even to emerge from behind her invented name. She's done the hard bit, she says, in writing the books. In fact, she's given wonderfully interesting interviews to both the *New York Times* and the *Paris Review*, which are without didacticism or self-revelation. But there are no photographs, no details. Her writing is very much a woman's writing, yet her alter ego in the book is given to repeating from time to time that women are men's invention and that there can be no escape from literary traditions that are mostly male. Education inserts itself between women's lives and their written accounts of those lives, encouraging them to accept condescension in men's valuing of what they write as no more than they deserve. Elena is grateful for her education and her reading. They have allowed her to write, and writing for her is the only way she knows to contain and even counter violence, disorder, unruliness. Yet she also knows that if her friend Lila were to write her version of a woman's life and experience it would outdo her own in some ways, would break through a self-imposed reticence and control to create something entirely new. Ferrante's four-volume Neapolitan novel contains both voices, Elena's and Lila's, in combination, in discord and separately. It is only with both voices, Ferrante seems to be saying, that the hidden and unruly lives of women may be heard and understood.

October 2015

Jeremy Corbyn

When, in June, Jeremy Corbyn managed to scrape together the necessary thirty-five MPs to back his candidacy in the Labour Party leadership contest, I rejoined the party. I thought then that he hadn't a ghost's chance of winning. It took less than a month to discover I was wrong, and that almost everyone else was too. Even Corbyn himself had said he'd only entered the race to 'broaden the debate'. Several of his original backers have publicly regretted doing so.

On the 12th of September Jeremy Corbyn collected 59.5 per cent of party members' votes, more than his three rivals put together: a landslide. And between May and September, Labour Party membership had grown from around 190,000 to 550,000.

I was one of the people who voted for Corbyn. We've been called 'morons', in need of 'heart transplants', naïve, backward-looking, endangerers of this country's economic and domestic security, unrealistic and, above all, young. Most of the parliamentary party Corbyn is now leading has recoiled from him as from a contamination: Hard-Left, Trotskyite, Bennite, Socialist, Pacifist, Vegetarian, even anti-Semitic and anti-feminist. Several ex-Shadow ministers refused to serve in Corbyn's shadow cabinet without even waiting to see if they'd be invited to do so. He will have a hard time leading his quarrelsome army of MPs and his somewhat variegated, though interesting, shadow cabinet. His most provocative appointment, of John McDonnell as Shadow Chancellor of the Exchequer, may well be his Achilles' heel. McDonnell is no fool, but he's given to splenetic outbursts, and apparently once said (as a joke) that he'd like to assassinate Margaret Thatcher. He hopes too for the end of capitalism.

It will be at least as hard dealing with a largely hostile press, which attacks Corbyn daily, in gigantic headlines, mostly for trivia: his clothes, his not singing 'God Save the Queen', his not giving a top ministerial job to a woman – though there are more women in his shadow cabinet than there have ever been – for not being sure whether he will kneel to the Queen, as he may apparently be required to do as a Privy Counsellor. He has unearthed a tie to wear for special occasions and he has abandoned his bike for the time being in favour of a chauffeur-driven car.

Polly Toynbee of the *Guardian* didn't vote for him, but I'm glad to say that she spoke sternly to her Labour friends in the Commons, advising them to knuckle down and work with Corbyn. He has been congratulated and welcomed by Tariq Ali and by former Greek finance minister Yanis Varoufakis, both of whom see his election as signifying something new, positive, hopeful in Western politics: at once critical of inert tolerance of inequality and corporate power, and focused on the needs and interests of the young and of the poor – both groups which have been badly let down by all the political parties in recent years and are understandably lukewarm about Westminster politics in general.

So far, Corbyn has done well. He is no orator, but he speaks simply and with conviction. His refusal to conform to the rowdy boys' playground of the weekly Prime Minister's Question Time was successful. Instead, he gently put questions to Cameron that had been sent him as emails by members of the public. Within his first week he has spoken movingly and sympathetically at meetings about the refugee crisis and has defended the trade unions and workers' rights, which are under ferocious attack from the Tory government at the moment. He is thought to prevaricate about Europe, and has indeed, as have some of his supporters, spoken at times of leaving the EU, as an undemocratic organisation. However, he is wisely keeping his counsel on this and insisting that Labour's stand at next year's referendum will depend on what Cameron achieves, if anything, in terms of workers' rights when he negotiates with Brussels.

There are many of us who find this a heart-warming and exciting moment, and also a surprising one. It is, of course, full of tripwires. Talk of a coup, of the parliamentary

Labour Party working to rid themselves of Corbyn well before the next general election in 2020, have dwindled somewhat; but there is still an abiding scepticism about Labour's ability to win an election under him. There is anxiety about the rough-and-ready organisation of his team: no visible spin doctors or advisors, no press officers, and not much lip-service paid to the party's internal traditions and hierarchies and management. He has, after all, spent almost thirty-three years as an MP voting frequently against his own party.

There is no doubt that this has been an earthquake for the Labour Party. It's the second earthquake of the year for them: losing the general election and losing their important and long-term foothold in Scotland was the first. The Conservatives have a small majority and considerable troubles of their own. The current state of the world hardly encourages optimism, but the changes we're witnessing here seem more promising than the vacuous political conversation we've endured for so many years.

November 2015

A European Reunion

In 1944, on the 26th of February, in the forests clinging to the steep sides of the Ardèche gorge in southern France, a confrontation between a motorised column of German soldiers and members of the local Resistance resulted in the death of one German. Six days later, the SS returned to avenge that death. The sixteen inhabitants of the tiny settlement of Hameau des Crottes – men, women and four teenagers – were lined up against a wall and shot, and their houses were pillaged and burned. No local people ever returned to the hamlet, and the event was referred to thereafter as the 'petit Oradour Ardèchois': a reference to the massacre of 600 civilians who were shot in the legs and then burned to death in the village of Oradour near Limoges, which has been preserved in its ghostly, ruined state to this day.

I'm just back from an idyllic holiday in that tiny village of Hameau des Crottes. Its huddled houses, built of local stone and so almost intact, have newly built roofs and wood and plaster interiors and a swimming pool and a tennis court beyond their outer walls. My family swooped like swallows into the village, by train and plane and bus and from far and wide: India, Tunisia, Morocco, Spain, Laos, Cambodia. The young ones woke late, stroked their phones and sometimes cooked for us all. The older ones swam, walked, played tennis, read and shopped in the charming markets, which were set up in a different village each day.

Travelling back on Eurostar, we were tipped out at Lille to go through French and British security, watched as we did so by armed teenage soldiers, with their guns at the ready. The train tore through the tunnel to avoid 'trouble' at Calais, where 3,000 refugees are crammed into a make-shift camp, from which they make dangerous and usually unsuccessful attempts to smuggle themselves into lorries or trains on their way to the UK. Passengers on other trains like ours had heard the worrying tramp and patter of feet above them as refugees risked their lives by climbing on to the roof of the train in the hope of reaching the UK by lying flat as the train went through the tunnel under the sea.

These contrasts are surely intolerable. We, who can travel the world, live, work and holiday more or less where we want to, are encouraged to 'debate' whether, where and how many refugees – people who, by definition, are not allowed to debate anything – should be allowed to have somewhere safe to live, to bring up their children, to work and play. It is impossible to imagine struggling to get your family out of terrifying dangers only to meet with suspicion and even with violence in the hoped-for 'promised land', and then be expected to await the result of a 'debate' conducted by smartly dressed men and women arguing in soundproofed rooms about how many of you may or may not be picked out and welcomed into Europe. Razor-wire fences and other hideous barriers have been erected to keep these 'marauding hordes' out; ostensibly away from the railway lines, but also out of our sight.

It feels like an irony that it is Germany which is ready to take by far the largest number of refugees, welcoming arrivals they see as useful, even necessary, to an ageing population, people with the energy and ingenuity needed to accomplish these hair-raising escapes from war and suffering. It is another irony that it is Angela Merkel who deplores the unwillingness of other European countries to take their share of refugees; that it is the German leader who reminds the others that if the European Union fails to uphold human rights in this direst situation, it is nothing, hardly worth supporting.

The UK, like everywhere else, has been shocked out of its reluctance to help by that small drowned boy found face down on a Turkish beach. One wonders whether our political masters would have been similarly shocked had he been black, or naked, or poorly dressed. But we should be grateful that if many of Europe's leaders are unwilling to commit themselves to anything more than the least they can get away with politically, many of the people they govern have woken up to the horror of what is going on. Even here, and even in Hungary, people are beginning to see that they must resist tyranny wherever it exists, and that to do so may entail acting against or independently of their elected governments.

December 2015

Paris

My parents escaped their families' disapproval by getting married in Paris and staying on as students: he of the piano, she of etching. Those were the first three years of my life, and when we got back to England I apparently spoke more French than English. My father never stopped wishing they'd stayed in France, even during the German Occupation, but we never lived there again, though we had French family holidays as soon after the end of the war as we were allowed to. I did a French exchange when I was sixteen, partly in the Place de la République and partly in Normandy; and then spent most of my gap year between school and university in Paris. So Paris has always been there across the sea, smaller and prettier than London, a whole day's journey away in the old days, with always the threat of sea-sickness. Now you get there between breakfast and lunch and can be back by teatime.

That's not all that's changed. It's said that there are half a million French people living in London now. They've come here to work, to shop, sometimes to study, and perhaps even for the food and the fun. The French no longer speak the comical English our films and plays so cheerfully ridiculed, while our public figures still make a point of speaking French as if it was really English. You should hear them intone the words '*Nous sommes solidaires*'.

And we should indeed show solidarity, if not quite as we're told to. Some of us may envy the French their republican faith in free speech and secularism, yet those ugly and offensive cartoons in *Charlie Hebdo*, the banning of Muslim women's dress and that triumphalist, arm-linking '*Nous sommes Charlie*' parade in January – its exclusions at least as manifest as its inclusions – have been, to my mind, needlessly provocative. But the truth is that both London and Paris (and indeed Brussels) are vulnerable in similar ways, and we are certainly no wiser than the French or the Belgians as to what should be done about it.

It probably makes little difference whether we add our planes to the French and the American ones that are already bombing civilians and making pretty limited impact on ISIS. We are bombing them already in Iraq, after all. But a passionate disagreement occupies our airwaves, in somewhat paradoxical tandem with news from the Climate Conference in Paris, about whether we should bomb Raqqa, and if so why. The city is full of civilians who have nowhere else to go, and surely the fighters will have the sense to move elsewhere. However, we're told that it has to be done (that it is, as they say these days, 'the right thing to do') in order to protect us from the sort of attacks Paris suffered. Yet most commentators here and in France who know about these things seem pretty certain that bombs, let alone more bombs, are unlikely to deter those furious young men and one or two women in large European cities from causing their particular brand of mayhem. The bombs might even encourage them.

A recent and rediscovered pleasure has been reading French. Laurent Bonelli and Olivier Roy, both writing in *Le Monde* and both knowledgeable about the character of these groups of angry and reckless young people, see their relation to religious Islam and to the so-called 'Caliphate' as not much more than a handy, identifying justification for their murderous activities: neither the source nor the inspiration for their rage. Their likely unemployment and a sense of futility and marginality in the cities where they've grown up, added to their alienation from parents and grandparents, who may seem to a younger generation to merge too compliantly with the host society, are seen by analysts like these as more effective recruitment mechanisms than ISIS.

Even the addiction of these groups to extreme violence may have its roots in video games almost as much as in the brutality displayed so graphically on ISIS videos. There are clearly differences that matter between those European young people who actually go to Syria to support ISIS or even marry into it, and those who stay in Europe and murder people indiscriminately: differences of motive and differences in the rallying causes that are invoked in justification.

Tomorrow our parliament will almost certainly vote to bomb a city full of people as 'innocent' as those who were killed in the Bataclan theatre, the Stade de France and La Belle Equipe and Carillon restaurants. Who will stop them?

December 2015

Mortality

For a whole year my husband Karl's ashes have been tucked into a tasteful maroon box and matching carrier bag and then hidden from view in another box by my front window. I'd sometimes have to nudge the box aside as I opened the window to water the flowers on the windowsill, and I always apologised to him as I did so. And then on the anniversary of his death the whole family and some friends made their way to Edinburgh where Karl grew up and to the Pentland Hills to the south-west of the city. And there we scattered his ashes, handfuls of silvery sand, among the Scotch pines. They rose magically in the air before disappearing in little puffs of smoke. The sun had shone in the morning, but, true to form, there was rain for our scattering. Making our way down the hill afterwards we were surprised and overtaken by a group of merry soldiers, who seemed to us unexpectedly drunk and oblivious. We were all curiously elated.

No one can say we haven't been warned that we're mortal. Christopher Hitchens wrote the essays in *Mortality* in the year he knew was his last, 2011, and Clive James has publicly eaten humble pie for announcing his imminent death more than a year ago and being still – embarrassingly – alive. Now I'm reading *Being Mortal* by the good doctor Atul Gawande, whose Indian grandfather lived to be nearly 110, cheerfully dominating his family while relying on their constant and necessary support. The book is a bestseller here, and it is in its way an inspiration.

It's not that Gawande expects Western families to

emulate his Indian one. He knows we're bad at mixing the generations, let alone acknowledging the pre-eminence of the oldest family member. What he wants is to disabuse us of the idea that medicine can always make things better. We should stop expecting to be cured of most things when we're old. Doctors, he writes, 'have reached the point of actively inflicting harm on patients rather than confronting the subject of mortality'. We must learn to talk about dying, so that we can work out how to live as well as we can under the circumstances. That seems both right and impossibly difficult.

We're bound, Gawande tells us, to lose quantities of muscle strength and of sight and hearing and brain cells and mobility in old age, and he doesn't spare us the details of the appalling illnesses and their depredations that are likely to assail us as well. He's given me such a fright that I made a rare visit to my doctor the other day to check that the moles on my arms were not cancerous (they aren't and are apparently standard old-age stuff), and I now walk to the swimming pool with my eyes permanently directed at the pavement for fear that I will trip over a child or a dog and tumble to the ground as he describes so many of his ancient patients doing. His enthusiasms for what can be done to mitigate these horrors can be rather terrifying too. Imagine having to assemble a flatpack birdcage that will house a pair of parakeets, in order that they may henceforth share your relatively limited living space in a new-age old people's home. That is what happened to a houseful of sad old people in upstate New York, who, at the benevolent mercy of a wildly encouraging innovator, were also introduced to a menagerie of dogs, cats, rabbits and chickens. However, Gawande manages, just, to wipe the smile off my face and even mitigate my scepticism by insisting that the inmates of that particular home were wonderfully cheered by their chirruping birds and their dog walks.

It may be Gawande who has inspired me to join a French conversation class, which has meant taking a test to discover my level of fluency. The questions you had to answer on the computer were mostly about feminism and green politics, so that though I had to beg for help with the strange Apple screen, I did surprisingly well. The danger is that I did so well that I may have to join a group of international bankers and that won't be much fun. But a proper conversation with a real live Frenchwoman afterwards meant that I now know the French for scattering ashes. You don't disperse them, as I'd thought. You *éparpilles les cendres*. And now I've started to miss Karl's ashes.

January 2016

An Interview with Tony Benn

Tony Benn died in 2014 at the age of eighty-eight. I interviewed him two years before that about his career as a Labour MP and cabinet minister. He left parliament ten years ago, announcing that he was doing so 'in order to spend more time on politics'. His political career, which began in 1950, was briefly interrupted in the 1960s, when his father died and he succeeded to the title of Viscount Stansgate. After a famous struggle, in which his determination to relinquish his title won popular support, the law was eventually changed so that it was possible to renounce inherited titles. Doing so, in his case, meant that he could return to parliament as a commoner.

Benn served during Harold Wilson's and James Callaghan's Labour governments, first as Postmaster General, then as Secretary of State for Industry and, later, Secretary of State for Energy. He moved leftwards throughout his life, and while this may have frustrated his ministerial career, he remained an enormously popular figure with Labour activists. Indeed, the adjective

'Bennite' has been used to describe the small number of left-wing Labour MPs and the much larger number of unhappy Labour supporters who have nonetheless maintained their loyalty to the party. The central belief for which he fought and argued most effectively was genuine democracy. Following his retirement he continued his involvement in grass-roots campaigns and politics, served as president of the 'Stop the War Coalition' and spoke warmly in favour of the Occupy movement. Eight volumes of his political diaries have been published. I expect that he'd have been pleased and astonished to see his old friend Jeremy Corbyn become leader of the Labour Party. My grandson Joe came with me to record the interview.

JM: I'd like to talk about your career and I'd like to talk about writing diaries, which you've done all your life, and about the Labour Party, but I do want to start with Occupy. Because I know you went there, didn't you, last week? And we went there last week, and Joe's been several times. And I wondered what you thought about it as a movement, but also what you said to them?

TB: It's a very interesting development, and it's been taken quite seriously, much to my surprise, because normally something like that would be dismissed. But it's hit at exactly the right moment – there's a major economic crisis in Europe and in the world. And these people have come out with a monologue we've seen on the tent and the flag: 'What would Jesus have done?' That registers quite well. And they're a very decent, quiet group – I've spoken to them a couple of times. There were about two or three thousand people when I went last week. They're talking about the nature of capitalism and the fact that it's a threat to democracy. In Greece and Italy the prime ministers have been imposed from business outside, and all the business news is about profitability, which leaves out other factors like homelessness and poverty. They have made a very powerful case, even though they've raised questions rather than found answers. And now that the American police are driving them off the streets of New York – and the same is likely to happen this afternoon here – I think it will stimulate interest.

JM: You don't think it will kill it? You think it's going to take off now?

TB: The way the establishment deals with new ideas is first of all they ignore them, and then if you go on they say you're mad, and after a while they say you're dangerous – and then there's a pause.

JM: But is it enough? People seem bewildered by the gentleness of it. And then there's the fact that the clergy are having their battles behind the doors of St Paul's – and that's interesting in itself, the fact that the Church has been stirred up. Lucky break, in some ways, for the camp, wasn't it? But what next, what are we in for?

TB: Well, it makes people think. Look at the situation thirty years ago, when the Soviet Union – which had seemed so strong and such a challenge to capitalism – collapsed; within a matter of weeks, the cruellest market society sprang up. At the time, this was seen as a great turning point of market capitalism in an incomparable crisis. There's no telling what will happen with Occupy, but it could be a sort of British Spring, like the Arab Spring.

JM: Paradoxically, almost the other way around, isn't it? I mean, I'm not sure that those young Arabs want capitalism, but they want what we've got. There's an interesting line in Eric Hobsbawm's latest book, and I thought I'd quote it to you. He says, 'The mechanism of capitalist growth generates internal contradictions, endless bouts of tensions and temporary resolutions – growth leading to crisis and change.' And in a way, we've got used to that cyclical business, haven't we? I suppose the question is now: is this cyclical or part of a series or is it terminal? Are we actually facing something we haven't experienced before, which is quite new?

TB: It may be the end, though I think that's unlikely. But it could be a moment when people who haven't thought very seriously about alternatives begin to think about them. And then campaigns to organise for change will take place, and some change will occur. If you look at our history we've had so many periods when there have been changes – the English Revolution, the Tolpuddle Martyrs and the suffragettes – when really big changes were brought about by pressure. So this may be one of those periods, but you can't forecast them.

JM: You've always pointed to the pressure exerted by big business and banks on governments, on political parties. Is it a different kind of pressure now? This idea of 1 per cent versus 99 per cent, this feeling that the banking world has completely run away with itself?

TB: The people that campaigned for the vote argued a similar line, saying we are being ignored by the government. All campaigns for change begin at the bottom and inch towards the top. It's not really a civil war between two parts of the establishment. It's much more of a challenge from the masses against the ruling class.

JM: A book came out recently, *Chavs*, written by a young man called Owen Jones.

TB: I know Owen Jones, but I haven't read it.

JM: It's an interesting book. He's a young man – looks about sixteen, but he is in fact twenty-seven – and his line is that the Left has forgotten about class and therefore poverty and inequality. For about twenty years we've been thinking in terms of identity politics, and that has distracted us from huge inequalities.

TB: Yes. It hasn't been articulated very clearly, but if you talked about class years ago, they said you were a communist, or a crypto-communist or a fellow traveller.

JM: Or that you were envious. To talk about class was to upset the apple cart and to express some sort of personal vindictiveness. Funnily enough, people don't now talk about class – they talk about poverty and inequality. And that seems a great change.

TB: We talk about our own experiences, and if you're unemployed or homeless or very poor and you think about your own condition and you ask yourself 'why?', that drives you to a class analysis of a kind, even if it's not explicit.

JM: What do you feel about Europe nowadays?

TB: I have no hostility towards the Germans or the Italians or the French; the real problem of Europe as it is set up is the lack of a democratic basis. First of all, we weren't asked before we were taken in – we had a referendum later. Then there's the way it works – Europe is run by commissioners who are appointed, not elected. I used to sit on a committee with them, and I found it really quite frightening that bureaucrats should be determining how things are done. And now you see in Greece, they displaced the prime minister and put a former banker in, and in Italy they've done the same. So, it's a very empty democratic structure.

Its power rests on the German economy, and the Germans are reluctant to support everyone else. On the other hand, if they let it go, they know that the European dream that they took on board will have failed. It's not a very satisfactory set-up. I think there will have to be some instrument for bringing Europe together, but it will have to rest on popular consent.

JM: It wouldn't get much popular consent in this country at the moment if there was a referendum.

TB: Not from the way it is now, no. The Tory Party has a nationalist projection of it. And the Labour Party has quite a number of people who share the view that I put. Whether or not the thing will bust up and we will withdraw, I don't know – it's possible. I think it's not very likely to happen because it would disrupt trading relations.

JM: What if Greece, Ireland and Portugal, and even Italy, did withdraw – would the whole thing collapse? Would it be a tragedy if it did?

TB: The question is, would it contribute to the further weakness of our own economy, because the British economy is in a rather poor state. And if we lost our exports, or many of them, to Europe, that might drive us further into a recession. I think that's what Cameron and a lot of people will be thinking about. Also, a lot of effort has been put into the dream of a united Europe, and if it turned out the whole dream was false, that the whole thing was going to end in disaster, it would have a very demoralising effect.

JM: That was never your dream, was it?

TB: I was originally in favour of the idea of cooperation. And then the democratic argument became the dominant one and I campaigned for the referendums, and we lost that. So my feud has been a democratic one rather than an economic one.

JM: You led opposition to the war, and you were at the forefront of opposition to Kosovo and the Falklands and Iraq. I've wondered what you felt – given our response to the Arab Spring – about Libya and our involvement there.

TB: I heard the arguments for going into Libya – to prevent Gaddafi from slaughtering people in Benghazi and so on. And the Arab League supported it. I can understand that argument, but underneath it all I felt that this was an intervention in a Libyan civil war. And undoubtedly the NATO bombing was one of the major factors in the collapse of Gaddafi, because to have three of the most powerful air forces in the world going at you day after day after day, must have been the factor that brought Gaddafi to his knees. And

now he's gone, and I just don't know how it's going to
work out. I was no supporter of Gaddafi, but I wonder
if an intervention of this kind wouldn't be seen in
the third world as just another example of Western
imperialism.

JM: We knew remarkably little about his opponents, and
who they were. And we still don't know very much
about them: who their leaders are, whether or not
they are Islamicists. And that has seemed very uncomfortable, hasn't it, from the very beginning.

TB: They were presented as the little men standing up
against the dictator, and he *was* a dictator. But, as you
say, we don't know much about them.

JM: Some of them were clearly not little men. It's been
uneasy, though not on the scale of Iraq. Which brings
me to you and the Labour Party. You've stuck with
the Party through thick and thin. And a lot of it has
been quite thin, hasn't it?

TB: Ever since I left parliament, I've devoted myself primarily to campaigns: peace campaigns, the campaign
against the cuts. Because stretching from the Labour
Party there's a lot of people around, and you form
these little grouplets. And then they divide and fight
each other. And I think, if you can concentrate on an
issue then you can build support within the Labour
Party and outside it, and be effective. I also think the
issue campaigns are more likely to recruit support
from Labour and influence Labour.

JM: Many people of the younger generation shun the

Labour Party but could be drawn in through particular issues, maybe. We've got a coalition now; do you, in the future, imagine big parties whittling down?

TB: The Liberals have done themselves enormous damage by supporting the Conservatives. And when the next election comes I think a lot of Liberal candidates will be defeated because of that. There is a growing opposition to the government – and Cameron. I think he's under a lot of pressure. On the other hand, when things get really bad, people have a tendency to rally around the status quo to protect themselves. Even so, there's the possibility of a change in government, and if that happens, we'll be in a different ball game.

JM: What do you feel about the Labour Party at the moment? Is it holding up?

TB: Ed Miliband is respected. He worked in my office as a student when he was fifteen, and I followed him through. And although I disagree with a number of things he's said – he criticised the unions that were going on strike last summer, and I think that was a mistake. But on the other hand, he made a rather friendly noise about Occupy. You can't look for a perfect person. He's probably as good a leader as we could have now. Better than Blair, who was just the wrong man. New Labour was really a Thatcherite group – when Mrs Thatcher was asked about her greatest achievement, she said 'New Labour'. That said it all.

JM: In all those areas I'm interested in, particularly

education, they've been absolutely disastrous. The Tories started it, but Labour consolidated it.

I wanted to ask you something about writing your diaries. Have you written all your life, did you write when you were a child?

TB: I started when I was very, very young. When I got up and went to school, you know? And then I began doing it more seriously in 1940, just before I joined the Air Force. I kept a journal – a manuscript journal. You weren't allowed to keep a diary if you were in the Air Force in case you were captured and the Germans could discover things about your activities. Not that mine would have been very interesting. But I did keep it during the war. And then, when I got into parliament, I used to dictate it to my secretary. By 1956, I was dictating it on to tape. When I sent off the tape to be typed up it came to about 15 million words. Ruth, who is sitting there, has edited the whole series. What's published represents about 10 per cent of the whole thing. But about two years ago I was ill and I stopped doing it. If you're not in parliament, you don't pick up the gossip, so I'm not sure it would have been as interesting now as it was in the old days when you were involved in every detail. So, I've got one final volume of the diaries to publish and it will be from the election of Brown as Prime Minister until 2009. And then I've got to finish it up, so Melissa's interviewing me a bit, and Ruth and I have got to work out a sort of volume which will be three or four years of diary and reflections, then the rest will be, I don't know, an assessment – the last diary and an assessment.

JM: When you read your diaries, do you look back and think 'I recognise that young man', or 'what a silly ass I was'? Do you feel you've changed? Do you feel continuous?

TB: I've made every mistake in the book, and I'm not ashamed of making mistakes, because you learn from your mistakes. The thing I would be ashamed of is if I thought I ever said anything I didn't believe in order to get on. I hope I haven't done that. My book is full of my mistakes – they're all there.

JM: In what ways have you changed?

TB: As I got older, I began to see things in a different way. I realised that the Labour Party – which I joined when I was seventeen, thinking it was an instrument for change in society – had turned out to be a group of people with a better idea for running the status quo, when actually the problem *was* the status quo. Nobody ever talked about that; they just moved nearer and nearer to the centre. New Labour was the culmination of that.

Now, with Occupy and the crisis, what's clearly needed from the Labour Party is some idea of how we might change the system, and that takes us back to our roots, to our philosophy and to our socialist tradition. And I think that is happening through the campaigns for peace and justice and so on. People have begun to draw from their experience some idea that we need to go further than has ever been done in the past.

JM: I've always seen you as having a wonderful balance of optimism and scepticism. I mean, you are an optimist, aren't you?

TB: You have to be, because if you don't feel you can win you don't put the effort in. And the media is always pessimistic about every campaign – they say it won't work, it's not realistic, no one will support you. If the media can spread pessimism, they can damp down all the campaigns that might bring about change.

JM: I think that's very important. We are absolutely bombarded with pessimism, aren't we, most of the time. I mean, simply to read the *Guardian* in the morning— it's a knockout, really. By about 8 o'clock, you've heard your fate, haven't you?

TB: Hope is the fuel of progress. In every human being since the beginning of time there have been two flames burning: the flame of anger against injustice, and the flame of hope that you can build a better world. My job is to go around fanning both flames as hard as I can.

JM: Is it different doing that outside a political party? Outside parliament?

TB: I've been very, very busy. I've been to a lot of meetings – last night, I was in Cambridge talking to some students at Peterhouse, and tomorrow I'm going to Reading to do a reading. I do a lot of meetings – peace meetings, anti-cuts meetings, trade-union meetings and student meetings. And, from all these events, I learn a lot, because people's questions are very, very perceptive. Public intelligence is far greater than the establishment or political leaders imagine.

JM: And they come in droves to hear you?

TB: Lots of people turn up, yes. The number of meetings that have been organised and the quality of the discussion nowadays is far higher than it's been for a long time. In the old days it was just niggling between the two political parties. Now there is some serious discussion being encouraged with very thoughtful people taking part.

JM: Is it about things like the Arab Spring and the economic situation, or inequality?

TB: The Arab Spring is an interesting example because that is a big moment of change for the Arab world, brought about very largely by the conditions – and the fact that you can pick up information on the net and therefore you are not dependent simply on some dictator's propaganda machine. That has had an effect in Britain as well. Sometimes I wonder if we're not having the British Spring right now.

JM: It must be very important for you to stay in touch with the young. Do you find that invigorating?

TB: I do find going to meetings exciting, mainly because the questions are so good. I've learned more from going to meetings than almost any other way. Someone sitting in the third row puts a tremendously profound question – and you have to think it out. And then the audience reaction guides you towards it. I think living exchanges are the most important thing, and that's what I enjoyed about being an MP: meeting constituents.

JM: Are you nostalgic about the past?

TB: As you get older you start to look back at the past in a slightly more remote way. You think of the mistakes you've made, and wonder why. You think of the possibilities that did exist, that you didn't take. And then you look at the whole of human progress and see how you can advance it. Every generation has to fight the same battles again and again. There's no final victory, no final defeat for any idea. You draw inspiration from earlier campaigns and you try to apply what you've learned to the present situation. If you're effective, you may stir up more support.

JM: Does one become more tolerant of uncertainty as one gets older?

TB: I think so. Old age is a time of uncertainty in a way, that's where maturity leads you. Also, you don't want anything when you're old.

JM: I'm interested in the loss of covetousness. It *is* a loss, because covetousness must've spurred one on as a young person. I haven't got it any more.

TB: Age doesn't remove desire, it removes the capacity to do much about it. That gives you a certain freedom.

JM: Yes, I think it does. Curiously, not wanting things is rather a relief.

TB: And not wanting to be elected, I've found, has been a

relief. Because in the old days, when you were speaking, you were really saying vote for me because I've got the right ideas. Now, you're not saying that. And that's a great relief to me.

JM: You don't have to be right, do you?

TB: No, no, no.

JM: I can see that. Well, as a final gloomy point we might end with, are we seeing the demise of the welfare state? Because, however many mistakes you feel you were involved in — you and I have lived through the creation of the welfare state. Which we were really proud of and dependent on. And I feel that it is being unravelled.

TB: It is being deliberately privatised, along with health and education. People need to grasp the fact that the vote gives you an opportunity to create things that are not dependent upon the market. And that's a huge advantage to have — a democratically accountable public sector. I think that will probably come back again, because attempts to privatise the welfare state have met with a great deal of hostility from the organisations of health and education.

JM: Not enough from education, I feel. I thought Melissa's book was very timely, because most people don't seem to realise what's happening. They think so long as they've got a nice free academy down the road, what's the bother? But the reality is they've lost all control over who goes to it, who teaches there and what people get paid. Do you think that people will wake up to this in the way they seem to be waking up to the threat to the health service? The campaign about health has been very powerful.

TB: People who work in the public sector who are under attack see it as an attack on their jobs and security. That's rather different from having an understanding of the importance of the public sector.

JM: I certainly feel with education that parents don't quite realise what's being shot at. And partly they believe they've got a choice, and of course most of them have no choice.

TB: I remember during the war, on a troop ship going to South Africa in January 1944, some of us wanted to hold a meeting to discuss what was going to happen when the war ends. We needed permission, so I was sent to see the colonel in charge of troops – I was in aircraft second class at the time, which is the lowest rank – and I said we wanted to have a meeting on when the war ends, and he said, 'No politics in it, Benn!' And I said, 'Oh, no, no.' Of course, we had the most wonderful political discussion. One lad made a speech I've never forgotten. He said: 'In the 1930s we had mass unemployment. We don't have unemployment in wartime. If we can have full employment killing Germans, why can't we have full employment building homes, building houses, building hospitals, recruiting nurses, recruiting doctors, recruiting teachers?' That was the spirit that led to the 1945 welfare state changes in Britain.

Those ideas haven't completely disappeared. People still question why there's plenty of money for war, but not enough for peace.

January 2012

An Interview with
Eric Hobsbawm

I first met Eric Hobsbawm when I was a student in 1952. We had a cup of tea together on a balcony of the Cambridge University Library, and he told me about the work he was doing on bandits. He and his wife Marlene have been friends ever since. I interviewed him in early 2012, not long after his book, How to Change the World: Tales of Marx and Marxism, *came out. He was frail and ill when we talked, though wonderfully unstoppable, and he died later that year at the age of ninety-five. I suppose that Eric's optimism, and mine, about the changes heralded by these movements, looks forlorn only a few years later, but it seems worth returning to the hopes that were raised for a moment in 2011.*

JM: I read *How to Change the World* at the beginning of last year and looked at it again the other day and thought, 'What a year it was, 2011. Everything under the sun seems to have happened.' And it's interesting that

the book is about how to change the world, how it has changed, how it might be changed. It seemed to me we might start off with those two possibilities of change, both the Arab Spring on the one hand and Occupy on the other.

EH: The Arab Spring is most encouraging. I didn't expect to see in my lifetime a genuine, old-fashioned revolution with people going on the streets and overthrowing regimes, something like the 1848 revolution, which is actually the origin of the name Arab Spring. Remember, 1848 was called the Springtime of the People. And whatever happens in the future is enormous. There have been a number of other positive developments, mostly because of the extraordinary ease with which it is technologically possible to mobilise young people – well, any people, but mostly young people because they are on the technological level. The Occupy movement is one example of this, as are the recent demonstrations in Russia. It is no longer possible to take the passivity of the citizenry for granted.

There are drawbacks to this. The people that take the initiative are not a highly characteristic or representative minority. They are the mobilisable minority, what I used to call 'the stage army of the good'; in this case, the stage army of the students and the bohemians. But the point is, if things go any further it will get out of their control – and it probably will get out of their control. Nevertheless, they are the ones that started it.

JM: The Libyan situation felt terribly risky and dangerous, didn't it? For a long time it seemed people might be simply mown down.

EH: One of the reasons I was keen to write this book was to keep reminding people, especially young people, that it is possible to change the world. If you are in a position to believe it's possible, you can imagine a different world and a better world and that does somehow give you a great deal of courage. Being heroic and brave is a fairly representative thing. Most people *are* under certain circumstances, particularly if they are with a lot of other people who are in the same situation. But it is incredibly impressive in a country like Egypt, where for weeks you had no idea whether they were actually going to send the troops out against you.

JM: You are good on generations. I think you have always had a good sense of what the young are feeling, what's possible for them. But, as you have already said, this group of young people are largely middle class and educated and possess technological expertise, but they are separate in many respects from any working-class or labour movement. Do you still feel that this is a middle-class kind of revolution?

EH: It's obviously something much bigger. Once it's big enough other people come in it.

JM: Yes, but it isn't fired by labour movements in the way things were in the past.

EH: No, but, just as in 1968, student movements set off quite large-scale labour movements in France and Italy. On the other hand, there is an undoubted danger of the division between people that get certificates in school and the people who don't. It's a division reactionaries know very well how to exploit.

JM: There is a tendency nowadays for the intellectual young to regard the working-class young as

reactionary and unreliable. I think of somebody like
Andrew O'Hagan, who has deplored the political
inertia of the English working class. Do you think
that's fair?

EH: Yes and no. Certainly it arose in the United States over
the Vietnam War, where on the whole the people that
went out to fight were working-class. And the people
that were getting degrees tried to get out of the fighting, not because they weren't heroic, but because they
disapproved of it. For the others, the appeal of patri-
otism was much closer.

JM: There has been a version of that vis-à-vis Afghanistan
and Iraq. Most of the young men and women who
fought there are working-class. You say at one point
that the trouble with middle-class revolutionaries is
that they are protesters rather than aspirers; clear about
what they don't want, but not about what they do want.

EH: It's also that certain issues are very powerful among
the educated middle class, for instance, environmental issues. If you say, 'What's more important in this
area, jobs or making it more green?' there would be a
difference in the class reaction. There are a number of
crucial issues for the educated minority, which is by now
quite a large minority, which don't have so much of an
echo among working-class people; for instance, a lot of
these issues on gender relations. I doubt whether you'd
find many branches of the GMB [General, Municipal,
Boilermakers and Allied Trade Union] passing resolutions in favour of homosexual marriage.

JM: One of the things that has happened in different parts of the world is the educating of women beyond the level of their husbands. At the time of the miners' strike in 1984, it turned out that a lot of the striking miners had wives who were secretaries and nurses and rather well organised and actually kept the thing afloat. That has always been a possibility in America and Eastern Europe; in countries like Moldova the men have to leave to become builders in other countries, and the women become teachers or nurses and to some extent form the educated middle class.

EH: That's true, and in some ways it's a very encouraging development because to move as it were from backwardness to modernity or poverty to wealth, one of the crucial elements is the education of women.

JM: That's been absolutely proved in India.

EH: Consequently the potential for mobilising women – and not necessarily only middle-class women – for progressive causes and for labour causes is quite great.

JM: Do you think that the kind of politics that went on in the 1980s, that some call 'identity politics', was undermining a genuine revolution?

EH: Yes, on the whole I do, because the politics for improving the world must aim at improving everybody, rather than a particular sector. If you concentrate exclusively – you can see it in the case of racism or nationalism – that is a very limited thing. And there are other, newer social movements that are geared primarily to their own particular interests and not to others.

JM: It's complicated because there is a moment when the focus on a particular group is important because otherwise it never gets aired. You could say that for a long time women didn't get a hearing among socialists; that didn't mean they should abandon the cause, but they had to assert themselves.

EH: There is a peculiar sort of paradox. On the one hand, socialists were very much in favour of the emancipation of women. Going back to the utopian socialists, they made a religion of it: women prophets. The most important writing by the working-class leader of the German Social Democratic Party, August Bebel, was about women in socialism. But when it comes to actual socialist governments and regimes, women have on the whole been under-represented. It was dramatically the case in early communist ones, but even in the social democratic Western ones the women had to fight for their position. On the other hand, women have always been absolutely essential to labour movements. Traditionally, labour movements have not been gender movements; they have been family movements.

JM: You've always thought, I remember you saying or writing, that the Communist Party was your family.

EH: Yes, but more than this I once did work on the origin of May Day. And the whole point of the May Day celebration was that it was a fiesta, a holiday. It was not just a political demonstration occupying the public space of the official regime, it was a family holiday. You could see it in the Italian Communist Party in the fifties: everybody was involved – men, women and children. To that extent, the family, which means basically the women, were absolutely essential. You could not possibly have a strike in a mine without solidarity with women.

JM: That was the case with the women in Barnsley: they kept the whole thing together, as secretaries and feeding people and so on.

But let us move on to the economy. In your book, you write about 2008 and the crash of capitalism in the West. You have a very good phrase for it: 'the jagged rhythm of capitalist growth produced periodic crises of overproduction which would, sooner or later, prove incompatible with a capitalist way of running the economy and generate social conflicts which it would not survive.' Jagged is very good there, isn't it? And then you talk about New Labour and a 'pathological degeneration of the principle of laissez-faire into economic reality'.

EH: It was pathological because it had no relation to reality.

JM: What happened to them? You knew Gordon Brown and spent some time with him at one point. What on earth went wrong with New Labour? I mean so very badly wrong really in so many areas, not just the economy.

EH: I do try and discuss this in the book, saying that the later decay of the twentieth century wasn't just the crisis of communism, but also the crisis of social democracy. Social democratic parties were parties for putting democratic pressure on their governments to reform this, that and the other. Once the governments lost control of their economy to a transnational economy, or didn't want to exercise it, these reforms became more and more difficult.

The last attempt to try and solve the problem of the economy within the borders of a middle-sized state was probably in France in the early 1980s, and it flopped very quickly. That meant even the moderate reformists were in a bind. And this is the awful business: they came down on the side of the pure laissez-faire people because they reasoned 'at least if these people earn a lot of money some of it will trickle down to us'. That was the New Labour line, really. Keep the City as important as possible. Don't start interfering with it because that is where the money comes from and if there are any kind of reforms to be paid for, that's where we are going to pay for it.

JM: Did you predict the sharp and sudden financial crisis in 2008?

EH: No, I'm not an economist. I had been predicting for ages that this triumph of ultra-neoliberalism simply cannot last. But I couldn't predict, I didn't predict, when it was actually going to break down.

JM: When you say it couldn't last, do you mean economically or socially or both?

EH: Economically. Sooner or later the thing was going
to crash. It was getting madly out of hand. Possibly
because I don't understand enough of the financial
side, and that was the side that proved to be the most
vulnerable, the one where the most short-term money
could be earned. But I don't think anybody really
expected it. Well, a minority of people expected it, a
small minority of businessmen. There is no question
about it, from 2008 on, it appears that the system was
no longer working. Back into depression and crisis.
It became clear this was the biggest crisis since the
1930s. It's becoming clear that it hasn't been overcome yet, at least in the Western countries. But at the
same time . . .

JM: It hasn't been overcome. We're in the middle of it,
aren't we?

EH: Also something has happened which is much more
serious. Capitalism has lost, has become conscious
that it isn't producing what it's officially supposed to
be producing.

JM: It's lost its nerve?

EH: In some ways. It's lost its sense of legitimacy. This
week, the *Financial Times* has a whole series on this
subject.

JM: It could only ever be legitimised because it worked.
There never was a moral argument for it other than
that.

EH: Exactly right. I think the thing that lost it was its public legitimacy and to some extent its legitimacy in its own eyes. This extraordinary polarisation of wealth, which created the Occupy movement, and which in turn meant the Occupy movement got vast echoes from other people who otherwise had no sympathy at all with anti-capitalist ideas . . . So for the first time in many years the question, 'Does the system require changing or such dramatic changing that it can no longer be regarded as capitalism?' has become part of the agenda.

JM: And, as you say, it's not just whether capitalism is the answer, but that it's become the question now.

EH: That's right. It's the question in itself.

JM: I don't want to go on exhausting you; you've spoken wonderfully on these issues. But one last question: is there anybody in politics at the moment who you have faith in and believe sees any of this, let alone could do anything about it?

A long pause.

EH: I must say I'm not very optimistic. It seems to me the basic problems which would have to be dealt with — economic problems, environmental problems, and others — are global or international. Globalisation has not affected politics. Even though the global organisations don't take decisions by themselves, they take decisions by agreement with their members. That's a weakness.

JM: And when you think that we are unable to confer on an equal footing with our European neighbours, this seems disastrous, doesn't it?

EH: Theoretically, it should have been possible for three or four major economies or states to come to an agreement. But even that does not seem to be the case.

The interview ended here, in mid-air. Eric was coughing badly.

March 2012

Illustrations

Acknowledgements

I must start by thanking Joel Bleifuss for inviting me to write a column for *In These Times* in the first place. I have felt lucky and privileged to be doing so. My son Sam has read every piece as it was written and has always given me helpful advice. I could not have dealt with the last four years without the love and support he, Georgia and Daniel have given me. Two of my grandchildren, Joe and Roxana, recorded interviews for me, and Larissa Gustova and Mariia Novikova were generous with stories of their recent lives. Brigid McEwen introduced me to the possibility of comedy in widowhood, while Diana Melly and Andrew O'Hagan have been encouraging readers and I thank them warmly. Lennie Goodings has amazed me by wanting to publish the pieces as a book and doing so with enthusiasm, and Tamsyn Berryman has been a vigilant and kindly editor.

In addition, I'd like to thank Flora Drew for the photograph of Ma Jian, Melissa Benn for hers of her father, Tony

Benn, and Rachel Dooley for help with pictures generally. Marie and Catherine Heaney, Marlene Hobsbawm, Hamish MacGibbon and Christabel Holland were kind enough to let me use family photographs of their own. My nephew, Tom Miller, took the photograph of my grandchildren, and Sam Miller took the photograph of Karl reading. Daniel Miller drew Karl, and my mother, Ruth Collet, drew me reading by an electric fire when I was sixteen. Andrew O'Hagan took the photograph of Karl's 'scattering'.

Index

virago

To buy any of our books and to find out more about Virago Press and Virago Modern Classics, our authors and titles, as well as events and book club forum, visit our websites

www.virago.co.uk
www.littlebrown.co.uk

and follow us on Twitter

@ViragoBooks

To order any Virago titles p & p free in the UK, please contact our mail order supplier on:

+ 44 (0)1832 737525

Customers not based in the UK should contact the same number for appropriate postage and packing costs.